CRYPTIC
SHAPE & NUMBER
CHALLENGES
TO BREAK
BREAK

Your

igloobooks

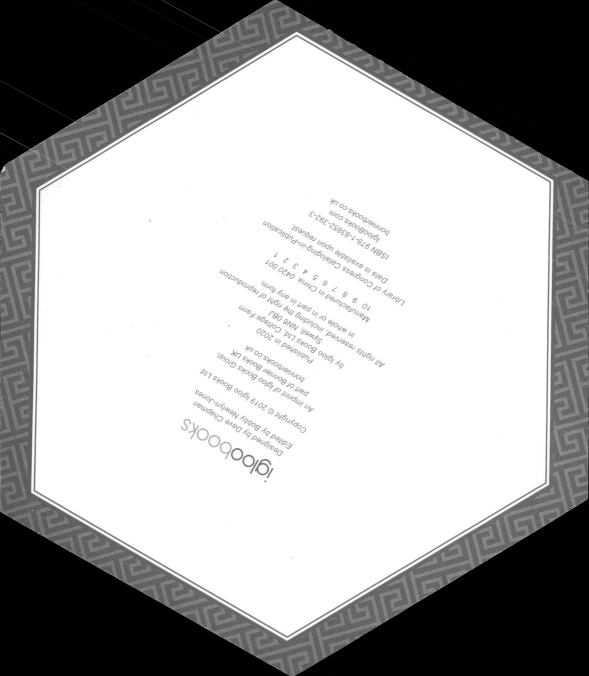

igloobooks

Designed by Dave Chapman
Edited by Bobby Newlyn-Jones

Copyright © 2019 igloo Books Ltd
An imprint of Igloo Books Group,
part of Bonnier Books UK
bonnierbooks.co.uk

Published in 2020
by Igloo Books Ltd, Cottage Farm
Sywell, NN6 0BJ

Manufactured in China. 0420 001
10 9 8 7 6 5 4 3 2 1

Library of Congress Cataloging-in-Publication
Data is available upon request.
ISBN 978-1-83852-392-3
igloobooks.com
bonnierbooks.co.uk

BOOKWORM

A student has read three-quarters of a geography textbook. She calculates that she has read 120 more pages than she has left to read. How long is the book?

A SPORTY CLASS

In a school class, one-sixth of the children prefer football. Double that number like swimming best. There are seven more children who prefer basketball than prefer football. Only one-tenth of the children prefer hockey. How many children are in the class?

SEQUENCE #1

What is the next number in this sequence: 0, 1, 10, 11, 100?

SOLUTIONS

BOOKWORM

240 pages; if three-quarters of the book is 120 pages longer than one-quarter of the book, then half of the book must be 120 pages.

A SPORTY CLASS

30

Write an equation where x is the total number of children in the class:

$$x = \tfrac{1}{6}x + \tfrac{2}{6}x + \tfrac{1}{6}x + 7 + \tfrac{1}{10}$$
$$\tfrac{7}{30}x = 7$$
$$x = 30$$

SEQUENCE #1

101

We are counting in the binary system.

MIRROR MIRROR

Find the pairs of mirrored pictures:

1
2
5
3
6
4
9
7
10
8
11
12

START WITH A SQUARE

Follow these steps:

1. Draw a square.
2. Turn the paper by 45 degrees then draw another square, centered on the same point.
3. Using straight lines, connect the corners of the squares through the center point.
5. Color in all the triangles.

What is missing from this sequence?

SOLUTIONS

START WITH A SQUARE

Step 4

MIRROR MIRROR

1:6, 2:11, 3:8, 4:12, 5:10, 7:9

PLAY DOMINOES

Arrange these dominoes in the three squares so that the sum of the three numbers along each side of each square is equal to the number in the center:

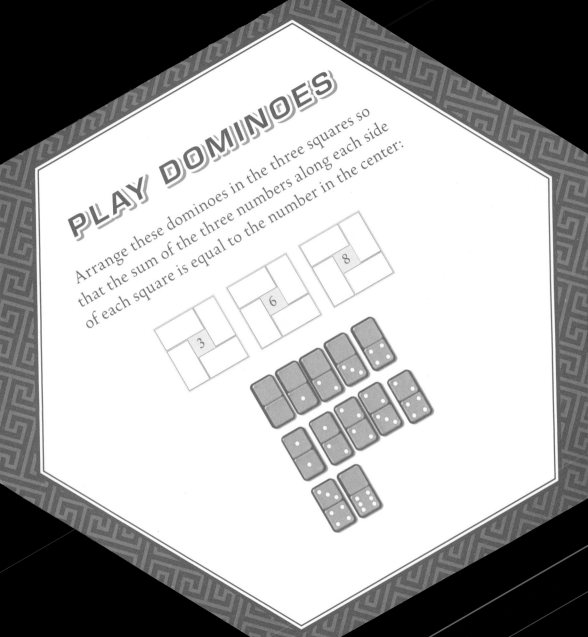

PLAY DOMINOES

This is a possible solution:

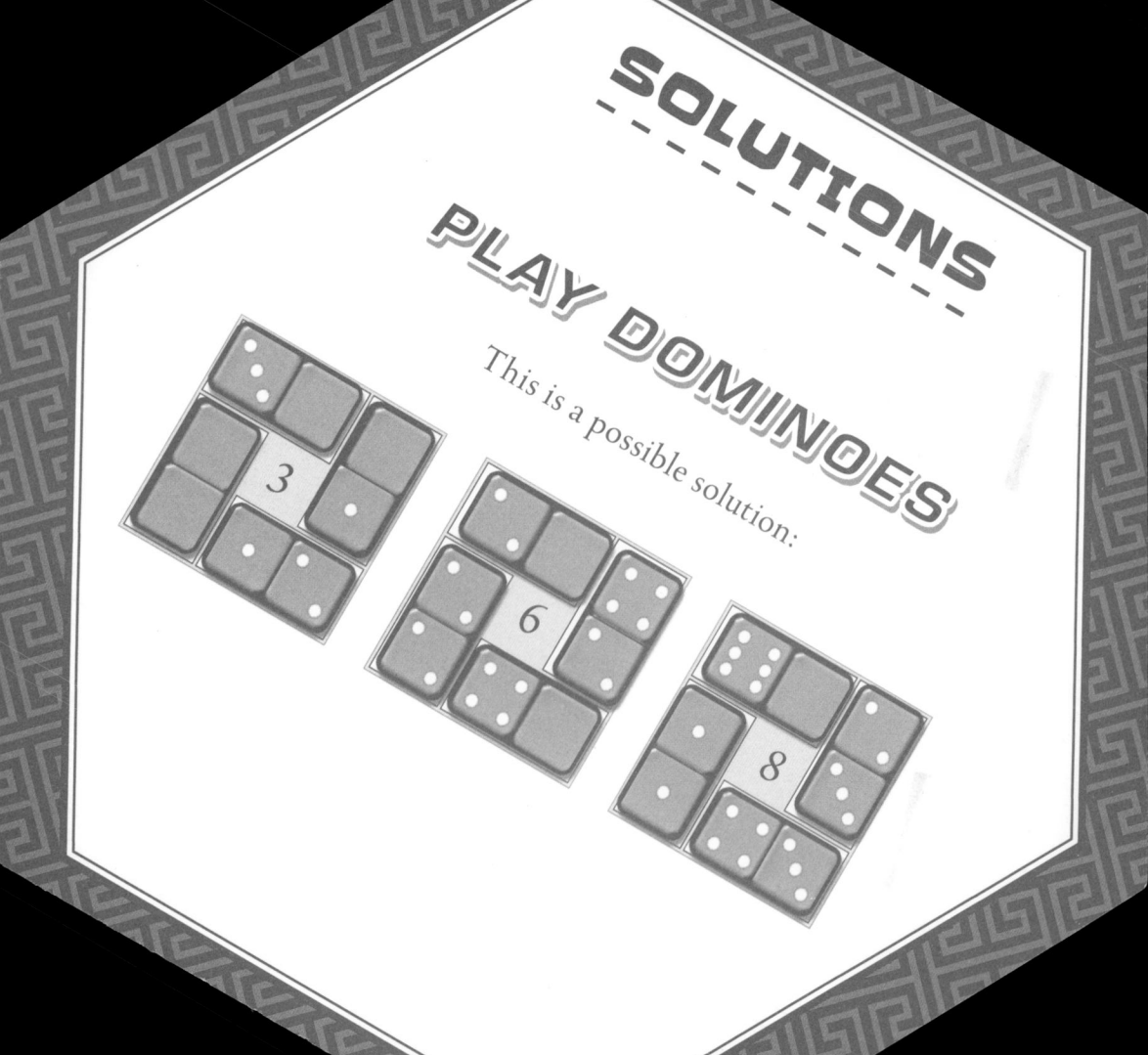

STICK SUM

Remove the sticks from this pile by removing the top one each time. What is the answer to the calculation you create?

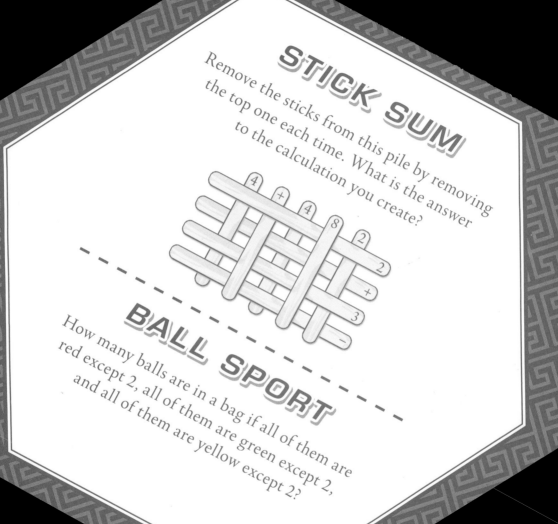

BALL SPORT

How many balls are in a bag if all of them are red except 2, all of them are green except 2, and all of them are yellow except 2?

SOLUTIONS

STICK SUM

114

The calculation is 82 + 32 − 4 + 4.

BALL SPORT

3 balls

There is 1 red ball, 1 green ball, and 1 yellow ball.

FINDING PAIRS

Find the pairs of frames that complement each other:

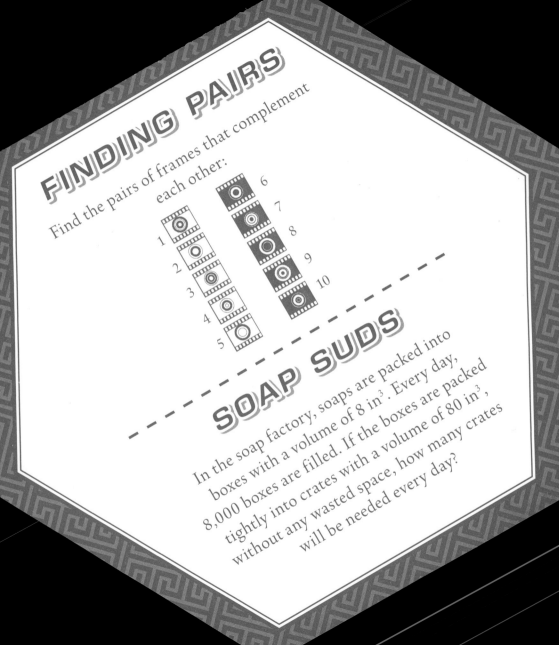

SOAP SUDS

In the soap factory, soaps are packed into boxes with a volume of 8 in^3. Every day, 8,000 boxes are filled. If the boxes are packed tightly into crates with a volume of 80 in^3, without any wasted space, how many crates will be needed every day?

SOLUTIONS

FINDING PAIRS

1:9, 2:6, 3:7, 4:10, 5:8

SOAP SUDS

800

If 10 boxes can go in each crate
(80 ÷ 8 = 10),
then 8,000 ÷ 10 = 800

MATCH-MAKERS

Reposition three of these matchsticks to form three squares:

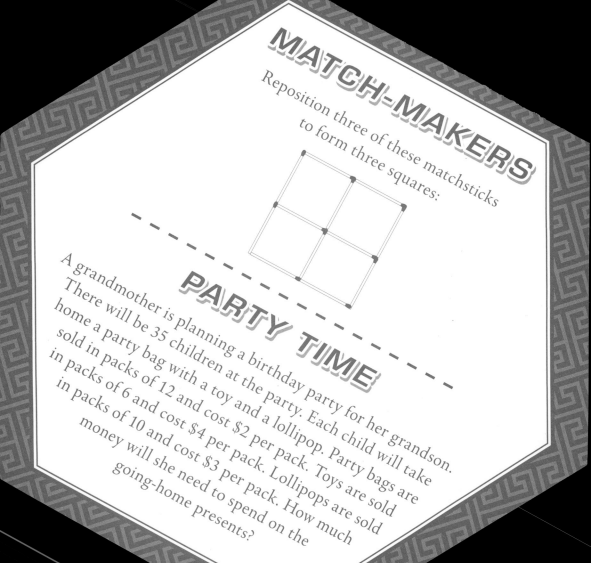

PARTY TIME

A grandmother is planning a birthday party for her grandson. There will be 35 children at the party. Each child will take home a party bag with a toy and a lollipop. Party bags are sold in packs of 12 and cost $2 per pack. Toys are sold in packs of 6 and cost $4 per pack. Lollipops are sold in packs of 10 and cost $3 per pack. How much money will she need to spend on the going-home presents?

PARTY TIME

$42

She will need to buy 3 packs of party bags, costing $6; 6 packs of toys, costing $24; and 4 packs of lollipops, costing $12.

- - - - - - - -

MATCH-MAKERS

SOLUTIONS

AGE RELATED

The sum of Maria's and her mother Gladys's ages is 99. Gladys's age is Maria's age reversed. Maria has just had a baby girl, Lucy. In a few years, the sum of Lucy and Gladys's ages will be 99, while Lucy's age will be Gladys's age reversed. How old is Maria now?

SHOPPING SUM

Agatha buys 4 items in a shop, each with a different price. She notices that the sum of the items' prices is the same as their product:

$$A + B + C + D = A \times B \times C \times D$$

If 3 of the items cost $0.50, $1.50 and $3.00, how much was the fouth item?

SOLUTIONS

AGE RELATED

Maria is 36. Gladys is currently 63.

In 18 years, Lucy will be 18 while Gladys will be 81.

SHOPPING SUM

$4.00

We can write this equation, where D is the cost of the fourth item:

$$0.5 + 1.5 + 3 + D = 0.5 \times 1.5 \times 3 \times D$$
$$5 + D = 2.25D$$
$$5 = 1.25D$$
$$1.25 \div 5 = 4$$
$$D = 4$$

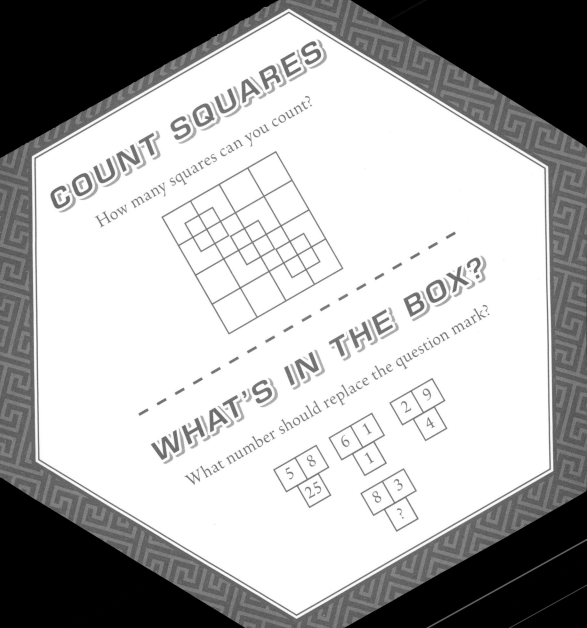

COUNT SQUARES

How many squares can you count?

WHAT'S IN THE BOX?

What number should replace the question mark?

5	8
25	

6	1
	1

2	9
4	

8	3
?	

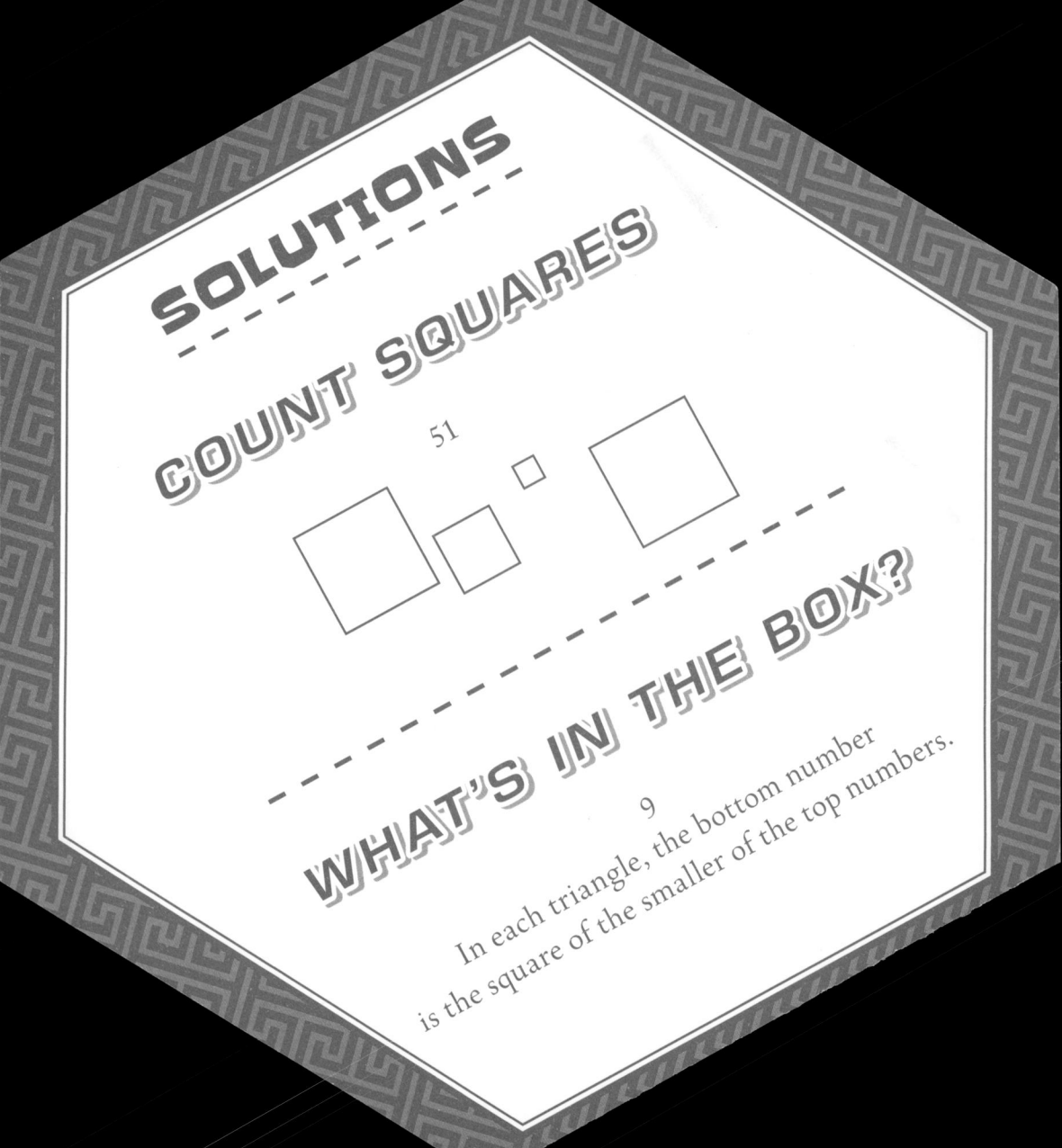

SOLUTIONS

COUNT SQUARES

51

WHAT'S IN THE BOX?

9

In each triangle, the bottom number
is the square of the smaller of the top numbers.

SEQUENCE #2

What is the next number in this sequence:

1, 4, 9, 16?

CLEANING UP

While his parents were away, Theo threw a party. It is 1 hour until they return and Theo must clean up the mess. He has to vacuum 8 rooms, take out 16 bags of trash and wash the kitchen floor, which he decides to do last. It takes 3 minutes to vacuum each room, 2 minutes to take out a bag of trash and 1 minute to wash each square yard of kitchen floor. If the kitchen is 2 yd by 6 yd, what fraction of it is still dirty when his parents return?

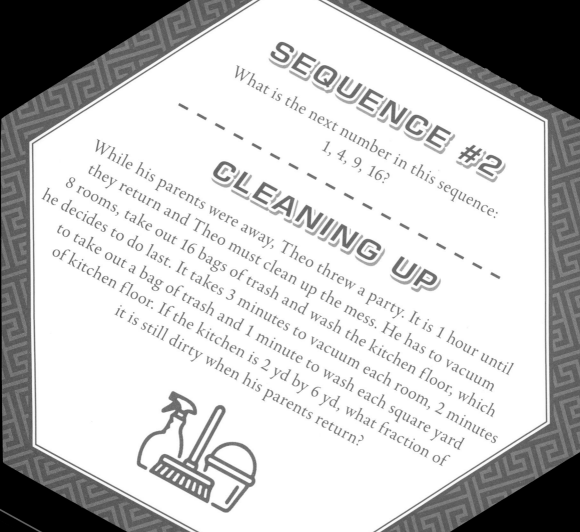

SOLUTIONS

SEQUENCE #2

These are consecutive square numbers.

25

- - - - - - - - - - - - - - - - - - - -

CLEANING UP

⅓ of the floor is still dirty.

Vacuuming takes 24 minutes, leaving just 4 minutes for the kitchen floor. The kitchen floor is 12 yd², which means that ⁸⁄₁₂ is unwashed.

SWAP CARDS

The children are swapping sports cards. They agree that 2 Cristiano Ronaldos are worth 1 Serena Williams, while 3 Usain Bolts will purchase 1 Williams and 1 Ronaldo. How many Williams can be bought with 6 Bolts?

FENCED OFF

A logician gave three friends some fence panels and challenged them to fence off the largest area using the smallest amount of fence. The first logician built his fence in a square. The second built her fence in a circle. However, the third logician won. What did she do?

HAPPY BIRTHDAY!

Agatha has just had her 100th birthday. Her son Joe is 76. How many years ago was it that Agatha was 3 times Joe's age?

SOLUTIONS

SWAP CARDS

3 Williams

We know that:

$2R = 1W$

$3B = 1W + 1R$

Therefore:

$6B = 2W + 2R$

$6B = 2W + 1W$

$6B = 3W$

- - - - - - - -

FENCED OFF

She built a small fence around herself,
then said that she was standing on the outside.

- - - - - - - -

HAPPY BIRTHDAY!

64 years ago,
Joe was 12 and Agatha was 36.

THE BREAD BIN

Professor Pi is making double-decker sandwiches for a party. Each sandwich is made of 3 slices of bread with 2 layers of filling. Each side of the bread that touches the filling must be buttered. Pi is making as many sandwiches as he can from 2 loaves, each sliced into 12, including the end crusts, which he discards. How many sides of bread must Pi butter?

- - - - - - - - - -

WHAT'S THE AREA?

This rectangle has been divided into four portions. You have been given the areas of three of the portions. What is the area of the fourth portion? You can find the answer without using complex formulas.

11	33
12	?

SOLUTIONS

THE BREAD BIN

There are 20 useable slices of bread, which will make 6 sandwiches. Each sandwich has 4 buttered sides (4 x 6 = 24).

24 buttered sides

WHAT'S THE AREA?

36 in.²

The top left rectangle has an area of $\frac{1}{3}$ of the top right rectangle (11 x 3 = 33), so it must fit into it exactly 3 times. The same must be true of the 2 bottom rectangles, so the answer is 12 x 3 = 36.

| 11 | 11 | 11 |
| 12 | 12 | 12 |

WINNING GAME

Clare bets two friends, Al and Bea, that if she plays three games of tennis against them, she will win two games in a row. They agree she must either play Al, then Bea, then Al; or Bea, then Al, then Bea. Al is a far better player than Bea. In which order should she play the friends to maximize her chances of winning?

AGING AMY

In 3 years, Amy will be 3 times as old as she was 7 years ago. How old is Amy?

FIGURE IT OUT

Replace the ?s with operators ($+ - \times \div$) so that the following equation is true (you may also add brackets):

1 ? 2 ? 3 ? 4 ? 5 ? 6 = 40

SOLUTIONS

- - - - - - - - - -

WINNING GAME

Al then Bea then Al. Although she must play Al twice, to win two games in a row she must win the second game. She gives herself the greatest chance of this by facing the weaker player second.

- - - - - - - - - -

AGING AMY

12

- - - - - - - - - -

FIGURE IT OUT

1 + 2 + 3 + 4 + (5 x 6) = 40

or

(1 x 2 x 3) + 4 + (5 x 6) = 40
(The brackets are not strictly
necessary in either case.)

IN A LINE

Four geometry students stand in a line, one behind the other. Each has a hat placed on her head, so the student at the back can see all the hats other than her own, while the student at the front cannot see any hats. They are told that one of the hats has a square on it, one a circle, one a triangle, and one a repeat of one of those shapes. Starting with the student at the back, they are asked to call out which shape is on their hat. Each does it correctly. How did they manage it?

- - - - - - - - - - -

FIND A 'Y'

Find the four Ys hidden among the Xs:

IN A LINE

The two hats at the front must have the same shape, so the student at the back knows there is only one shape remaining for her hat. The next student also sees the duplicates, so knows that the other remaining shape must be hers. The last two students realize that the first two students could only have duplicates, so know that they both saw duplicates, so know that they both must have the remaining shape.

FIND A "Y"

CLEVER MARY

Mr. Pompey's Latin vocabulary test has 10 questions. He gives 5 marks for a correct answer, deducts 1 mark for an incorrect answer, and awards 0 marks for an unanswered question.

If Mary gets 23 marks, how many questions did she get right?

- - - - - - - - - - - - - - - -

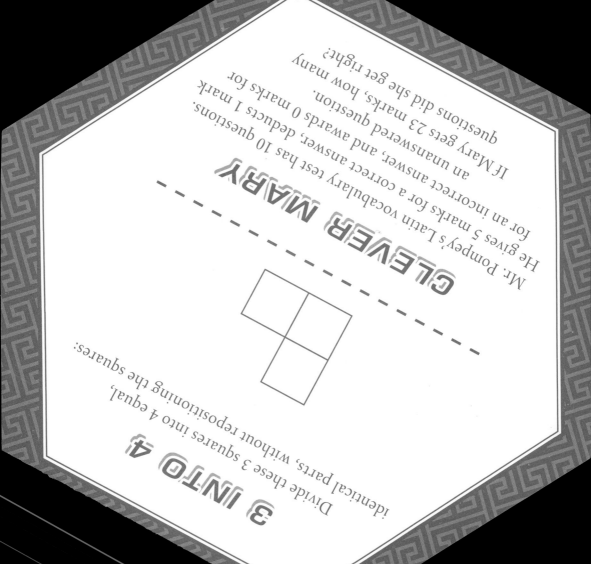

3 INTO 4

Divide these 3 squares into 4 equal, identical parts, without repositioning the squares.

SOLUTIONS

3 INTO 4

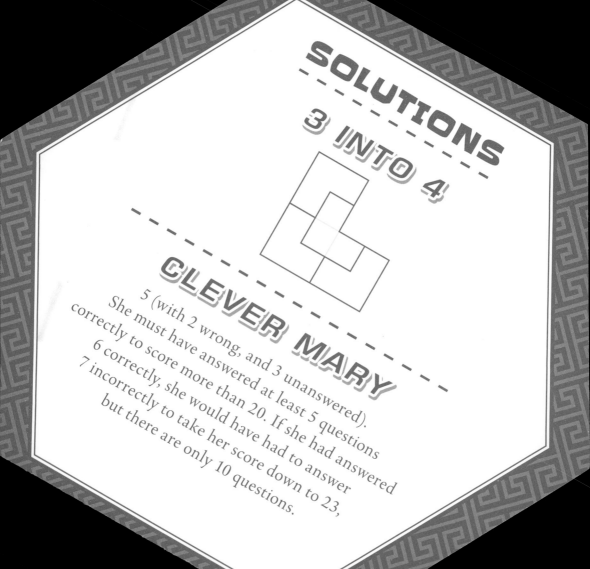

CLEVER MARY

5 (with 2 wrong, and 3 unanswered).
She must have answered at least 5 questions
correctly to score more than 20. If she had answered
6 correctly, she would have had to answer
7 incorrectly to take her score down to 23,
but there are only 10 questions.

100

Find a way to make the number 100 using the digits 1, 2, 3, 4, 5, 6 and 7 (in order) and only the + operator.

- - - - - - - - - - - - - - - - -

ALL GREEK

Professor Esperanto is planning a language conference for teachers of French, Greek, and Hungarian. The local schools have sent her a list of 40 teachers: 13 French teachers, 12 Greek teachers, and 15 Hungarian teachers. The problem is that they forgot to note who teaches which language. If Esperanto wants to be sure of inviting at least 1 teacher of each language, what is the smallest number of teachers she should invite?

SOLUTIONS

100

$$1 + 23 + 4 + 5 + 67 = 100$$

Or

$$1 + 2 + 34 + 56 + 7 = 100$$

ALL GREEK

29

Her first 28 invitations may be accidentally sent to all the Hungarian and French teachers (15 + 13) so she must send 1 extra to be sure of getting a Greek teacher, too.

SOLVE A SUM

Replace the ?s with operators ($+$ $-$ $\times$ $\div$) so that the following equation is true (you may also add brackets if you want):

$$1 ? 2 ? 3 ? 4 ? 5 ? 6 = 126$$

HOW MANY CHILDREN?

In his history class, Professor Herodotus notes the following facts: 15 of the children are girls; 9 of the children are wearing sweaters; 11 of the children are neither girls nor wearing sweaters; 5 of the children are girls who are wearing sweaters. How many children are in the class?

EGG TIMER

Humphrey would like to boil an egg for 7 minutes, but he has only 3-minute and a 5-minute hourglasses. How does he use the hourglasses to time 7 minutes?

SOLUTIONS

SOLVE A SUM

$1 + 2 + 3 + (4 \times 5 \times 6) = 126$

HOW MANY CHILDREN?

30

There are 15 girls (5 of them wearing sweaters) and 15 boys (4 of them wearing sweaters). There are then 11 children who are neither girls nor wearing sweaters, which brings the total of boys up to 15. Add this to the 15 girls and you have a total of 30.

EGG TIMER

He turns both hourglasses over at once. When the 3-minute glass runs out, he turns it over. Then 2 minutes later, when the 5-minute hourglass runs out, he turns over the 3-minute hourglass again. Finally, 3 minutes later, when that hourglass runs out, his egg is ready.

RED AND BLUE

In the ball factory there are three sealed boxes of balls. One box contains blue balls, one contains red balls, and one contains a mix of blue and red balls. Each crate is labeled: "Blue balls," "Red balls," and "Blue and red balls." However, the labeling machine has broken and is labeling every crate incorrectly. To correct the labeling, the factory manager wants to break the seal on one box and only remove one ball from it. What should she do?

- - - - - - - - - - - - -

RIGHT ANGLES

How many right angles can you see in this image?

RED AND BLUE

She should break the seal on the box labeled "Blue and red balls." If it contains blue balls, she will know this is the "Blue balls" box (it cannot be the mixed box because every crate is labeled incorrectly). Therefore, she will know that the crate marked "Red balls" must contain red balls and the crate marked "Blue balls" must be mixed. The reverse reasoning would be true if she pulled out a red ball.

RIGHT ANGLES

None

There are three diamonds, although you may imagine you are looking at a representation of a cube.

NUMBER FUN

Professor Logic writes down 4 whole numbers. The average (mean) of the numbers is 4. The difference between the smallest and highest numbers is 5. The smallest number is 2. She did not write down the number 3. Which numbers did she write down?

- - - - - - - - - - - - - - - -

NOT INSIDE, OUTSIDE

Reposition two matchsticks so that the flower is outside the same shape:

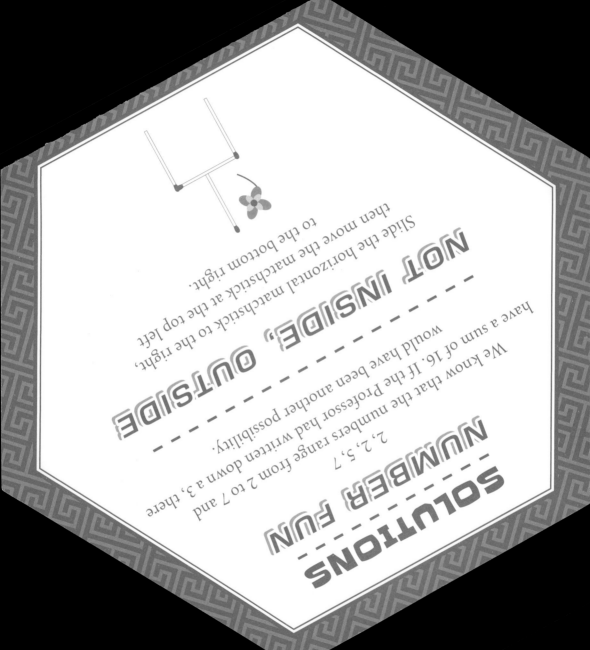

NUMBER FUN

We know that the numbers range from 2 to 7 and would have a sum of 16. If the Professor had written down a 3, there have a sum of 16. If the Professor had written down a 3, there would have been another possibility.

2, 2, 5, 7

NOT INSIDE, OUTSIDE

Slide the horizontal matchstick to the right, then move the matchstick at the top left to the bottom right.

EQUATION

Replace the ?s with operators $(+ - \times \div)$ so this equation is true: $10 \, ? \, 20 \, ? \, 30 \, ? \, 40 = 150$

ON THE BUS

At its first stop, 17 people get off bus no.186, but 19 people get on. At the second stop, only 3 people get off but 10 get on. At the third stop, 12 get off and 7 get on. How many were on the bus when it set off?

HOW MANY BUTTERFLIES?

There are 13 blue butterflies in the lepidopterarium. There are 12 female butterflies, while 7 green butterflies are male. There are also 3 white butterflies, which are all male. Of the blue butterflies, 6 are female. If there are only green, blue, and white butterflies in the lepidopterarium, how many butterflies are there in total?

SOLUTIONS

EQUATION
10 x 20 x 30 ÷ 40 = 150

ON THE BUS
40

HOW MANY BUTTERFLIES?
29

There are 13 blue butterflies
(7 male and 6 female), 13 green butterflies
(7 male and 6 female) and 3 white
butterflies (all male).

JACK AND JILL

Jack is three times as old as Jill. When Jack is double the age he is now, Jill's age will be two-thirds of his, but both their ages will still be in single digits. How old is Jack?

A, B, C, OR D?

Which shape is next in the sequence: A, B, C, or D?

SOLUTIONS

- - - - - - - -

JACK AND JILL

3

Jack is 3 and Jill is 1. When Jack is 6, Jill will be 4.

- - - - - - - - - - - - - - - - -

A, B, C, OR D

A

OPTICAL ARC

Which arc is taken from the largest circle?

DECK OF CARDS

Identify the cards using these hints:

There are 4 playing cards laid out in a row on a table.

1. Only 2 suits are on the table.
2. No card has a lower number than any card to its left.
3. There are no aces, jacks, queens or kings.
4. The difference between the first and third cards is 8.
5. The difference between the second and fourth cards is 7.
6. The 2 cards on the left are hearts, while the fourth card is a diamond.

SOLUTIONS

OPTICAL ARC

All the arcs are taken from identically sized circles.

DECK OF CARDS

2 of hearts, 3 of hearts, 10 of hearts, 10 of diamonds

Hint 2 tells us that the second and fourth cards must be 3 and 10 rather than 2 and 9 (since card 3 is a 10 and card 4 cannot be lower). Since card 4 is the 10 of diamonds, card 3 must be the 10 of hearts if there are only 2 suits.

SEQUENCE #3

What is the next number in this sequence:

3, 5, 8, 13, 22, 39?

CLIFFHANGER

A mountaineer climbs three-quarters of the way up a cliff, only to lose his grip and slip 20 ft down. He hauls himself up to a ledge 1 ft above. He climbs the rest of the way at a steady speed of 4 ft/min, taking 20 minutes. How tall is the cliff?

UPSIDE DOWN

How many circles must you move to turn this triangle upside down, so its apex is at the bottom?

SOLUTIONS

SEQUENCE #3

The sequence is x2 – 1, x2 – 2, x2 – 3, x2 – 4, x2 – 5, x2 – 6.

72

CLIFFHANGER

244 ft

One-quarter of the height is 61 ft: 80 ft (4 ft x 20), minus 19 ft.

UPSIDE DOWN

2

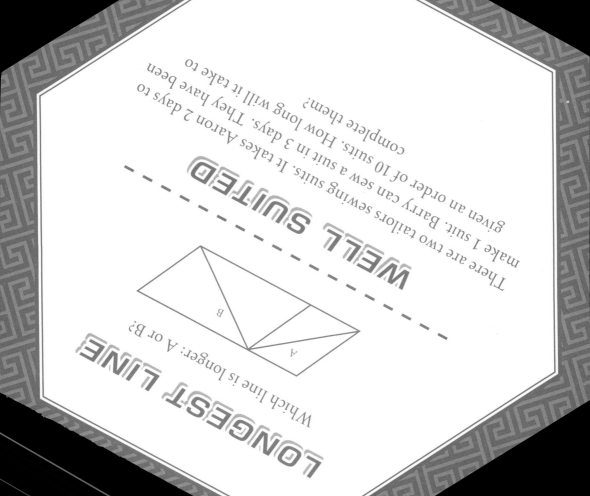

WELL SUITED

There are two tailors sewing suits. It takes Aaron 2 days to make 1 suit. Barry can sew a suit in 3 days. They have been given an order of 10 suits. How long will it take to complete them?

- - - - - - - - - -

LONGEST LINE

Which line is longer: A or B?

SOLUTIONS

LONGEST LINE

They are both the same length.

WELL SUITED

12 days

Aaron can complete 3 suits in the time it takes Barry to make 2, so Aaron will make 6 suits and Barry will make 4. It takes Aaron 12 days to make 6 suits.

THREE FIVES

How can three 5s equal 50?

BOYS AND GIRLS

In the nursery, there are 6 toddlers that are crying loudly. Exactly 7 toddlers are boys. There are 4 toddlers that are crying while 3 of the boys are crying. If 1 nursery worker is not allowed to look after more than 3 toddlers at once, how many nursery workers must be on duty today?

DRINKS?

At a stall in the park, an ice cream and a drink cost $4.10. The ice cream costs $1 more than the drink. How much does the drink cost?

SOLUTIONS

DRINKS

$1.55

BOYS AND GIRLS

5

There are 14 toddlers: 6 boys (3 of them are crying) and 8 girls (1 of them is crying).

THREE FIVES

$55 - 5 = 50$

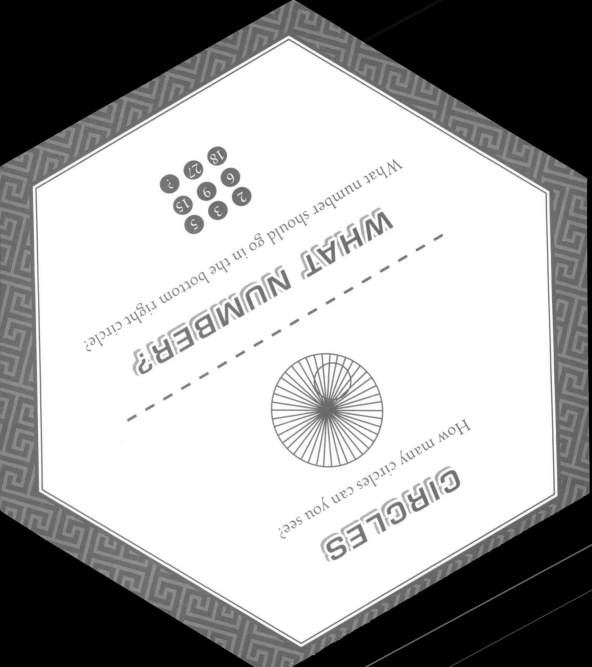

WHAT NUMBER?

What number should go in the bottom right circle?

18 27 ?
9 6
15 5
3 2

CIRCLES

How many circles can you see?

SOLUTIONS

CIRCLES

2

Despite what your eyes tell you, the shape to the bottom left of the center is a perfect circle.

WHAT NUMBER?

45

In each column, each number is 3 times the one above.

SEQUENCE #4

What is the next number in this sequence:

1, 16, 2, 15, 4, 13, 7, 10, 11?

TEAM GAME

Members of the baseball team want to play cards, but have lost some cards from their pack. Now, if the cards are dealt between 2 or 3 players, 1 card remains. If they are dealt between 5 players, 4 remain. However, if a different number of team members joined in, the cards could be dealt evenly. How many cards are there?

THE RIGHT DOSAGE

Angela has 2 bottles of identical-looking tablets. She must take 1 tablet from each bottle every day: if she forgets to take 1 or takes more than 1 of either, she will be ill. When she has 2 days' supply left, she drops all 4 tablets on the floor, mixing them up. What should Angela do?

SOLUTIONS

SEQUENCE #4

6

There are 2 sequences, running alternately:
− 1, − 2, − 3, − 4... and + 1, + 2, + 3, + 4.

TEAM GAME

49

Another option would be 19, but 19 cards could not be divided evenly among any fewer than 19 players (a baseball team has 9 players).

THE RIGHT DOSAGE

Angela should take half of each tablet today, then the other halves tomorrow.

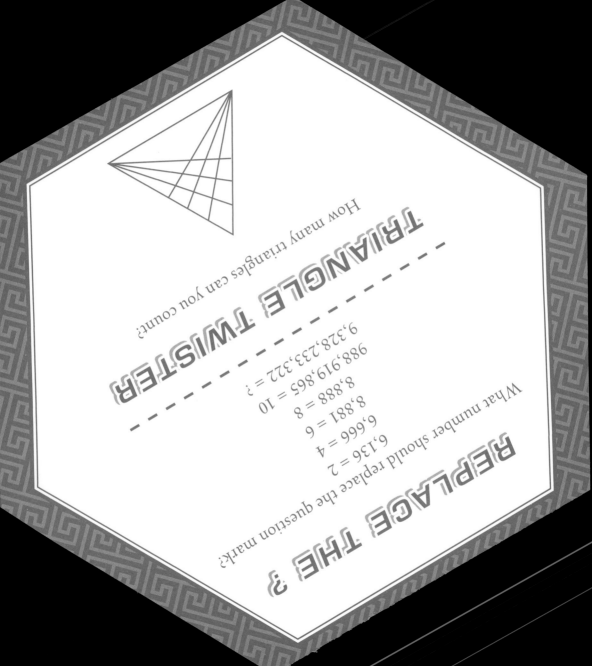

TRIANGLE TWISTER

How many triangles can you count?

REPLACE THE ?

What number should replace the question mark?

$6,136 = 2$

$6,666 = 4$

$8,881 = 6$

$8,888 = 8$

$988,919,865 = 10$

$9,328,233,322 = ?$

REPLACE THE ?

3

We are counting the number of enclosed spaces,
so 6 = 1, 8 = 2 and 9 = 1.

TRIANGLE TWISTER

64

JANUARY 1

January 1, 2002 – or 1/1/02 – was the first day in the 21st century when the sum of its day and month added up to its year $(1 + 1 = 2)$. What will be the last day of the 21st century when this will be the case?

- - - - - - -

FILLING A SANDPIT

A park keeper needs to move 200 lb of sand out of the old sandpit and into a new one. Every day, she can carry 50 lb of sand. The new pit is in a windy spot, so every night 10 lb of sand blows off its surface. How many days does it take the park keeper to fill the new sandpit?

which has room for only 170 lb of sand,

SOLUTIONS

JANUARY 1

December 31, 2043

Both the month (12) and day (31) are as big as possible.

FILLING A SANDPIT

4 days

At the start of the second day, there is 40 lb of sand in the new pit; at the start of the third, there is 80 lb; at the start of the fourth, there is 120 lb. The park keeper fills the new pit with 170 lb of sand by the end of the fourth day (even though 10 lb of sand will blow away later that night).

LIFE OF ELSPETH

Elspeth finished school after she had lived one-fifth
of her life. After one-eighth more of her life,
she got married. Then, 4 years later, she had a son.
Her son lived one-half as long as his mother.
Elspeth died 10 years after her son.
How long did Elspeth live?

SHAPE SHIFTER

Which shape is next in the sequence: A, B, or C?

I CAN'T DO
EVEN ONE
😊
Grace M
2022

SHAPE SHIFTER

A

LIFE OF ELSPETH

80 years

We can write this equation, where x is Elspeth's lifespan:

$$\frac{1}{5}x + \frac{1}{8}x + 4 + \frac{1}{2}x + 10 = x$$

$$\frac{1}{2}x - \frac{1}{5}x - \frac{1}{8}x = 14$$

$$\frac{7}{40}x = 14$$

$$x = 80$$

FIND THE TWINS

Which two squares have identical sets
of signs on them?

SOLUTIONS

FIND THE TWINS

6 and 11

OUT OF GAS

Professor Benz drives home from holiday.

He sticks to exactly 60 mph and manages 20 miles per gallon of gas. At the start of the journey, he has 16 gallons in his tank. His car is leaking gas at a rate of 1 gallon per hour. He arrives home just as he runs out of gas.

How far did he drive?

- - - - - - - - - - - - - - - -

SHAPE SUM

What numbers do the squares, circles, and triangles represent?

$$\square \bigcirc \triangle + \square \bigcirc \triangle + \square \bigcirc \triangle = \triangle \triangle \triangle$$

- - - - - - - - - - - - - - - -

SEQUENCE #5

What is the next number in this sequence:

41, 43, 47, 53, 59?

SOLUTIONS

OUT OF GAS

240 miles

He was driving at 60 mph at a rate of 20 mpg, so he was using 3 gallons of gas every hour. He was also losing 1 gallon every hour. To use the 16 gallons in the tank, he must drive for 4 hours. At 60 mph, this means he drove 240 miles.

SHAPE SUM

$\square$ = 1, $\bigcirc$ = 8, $\triangle$ = 5

185 + 185 + 185 = 555

SEQUENCE #5

61

This is a list of prime numbers, starting with the first prime number over 40.

GOOD NEIGHBORS

Joe and Jules live on the same street. Their ages contain the same 2 digits, but reversed. The difference between their ages ends in 2. What are their lowest possible ages?

COMPLETE CUBE

Which shape completes the cube: A, B, or C?

SOLUTIONS

COMPLETE CUBE

C

GOOD NEIGHBORS

19 and 91

This is best arrived at by trial and error.

TRIANGLE TEST

How many triangles can you count?

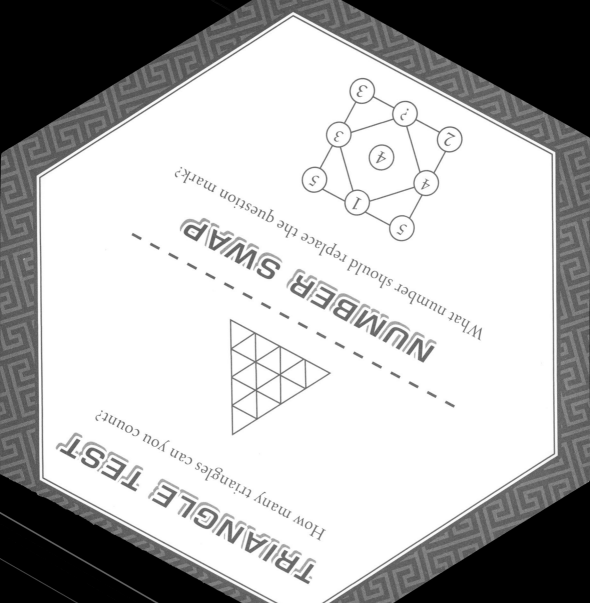

NUMBER SWAP

What number should replace the question mark?

SOLUTIONS

TRIANGLE TEST

27

NUMBER SWAP

6

Each row and column adds up to 11.

SEQUENCE #6

What is the next number in this sequence:

699889, 49, 13?

A QUESTION OF NUMBERS

What number should replace the question mark?

EMPTY POOL

Water drains out of a swimming pool at a rate of 1,000 ft³ every 4 hours. It takes 10 hours to drain the pool. How much water was in the pool?

SOLUTIONS

EMPTY POOL

2,500 ft³

If the total time was 10 hours, the amount of water is 1,000 ft³ x ¹⁰⁄₄ (or x2.5).

A QUESTION OF NUMBERS

16

(2 x 3) + (3 x 4) = 18
(1 x 2) + (3 x 4) = 18
(1 x 4) + (2 x 3) = 7
(1 x 4) + (1 x 2) = 6
(1 x 4) + (3 x 4) = 16

SEQUENCE #6

4

Each number is the sum of the digits in the previous number.

COUNT SQUARES

How many squares can you count?

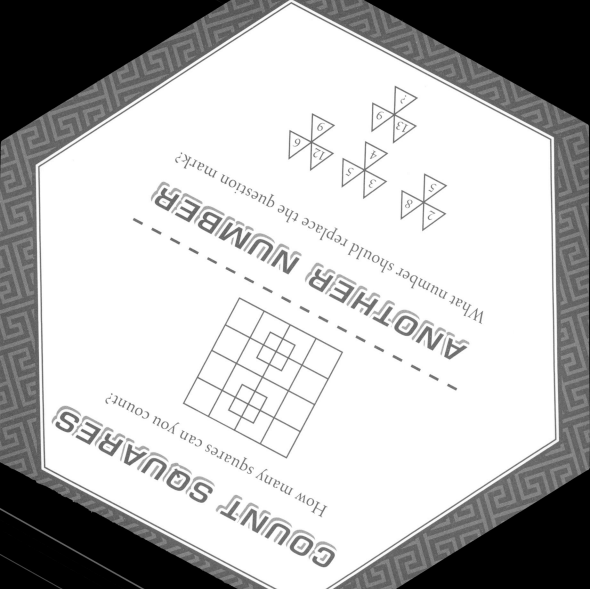

- - - - - - - - -

ANOTHER NUMBER

What number should replace the question mark?

COUNT SQUARES

40

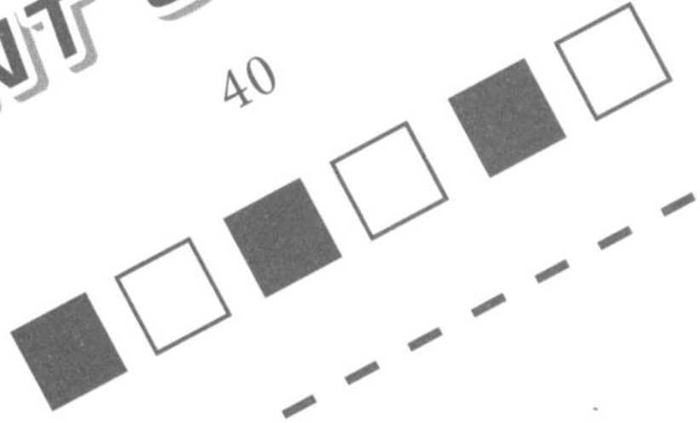

ANOTHER NUMBER

11

In each set of triangles, the bottom number is the average of the top 2 numbers.

SEQUENCE #7

What is the next number in this sequence:
99, 20, 97, 22, 95, 24, 93, 26?

TEA AND COFFEE

In a coffee shop, there are double the number of women as men. The number of women drinking tea is double the number of men drinking tea. The number of men drinking tea is double the number of men drinking coffee. The number of people in the coffee shop is between 20 and 30. How many customers are there?

SOLUTIONS

- - - - - - - -

TEA AND COFFEE

27

The number of men must be a multiple of 3 as they can be split in the ratio 2:1 (tea:coffee). There must be 3, 6, 9, or 12 men, while there are double that number of women: 6, 12, 18, or 24. If the total is above 20 but below 30, the only solution is 27 (9 men and 18 women).

- - - - - - - -

SEQUENCE #7

91

There are 2 sequences, running alternately:
99, 97, 95, 93, 91...
and 20, 22, 24, 26.

A LOT OF FOOD

A father is planning his daughter's party. He knows he will need 60 bowls to fill with food according to this plan:

1. Each child will have their own bowl of pasta.
2. Every 2 children will share a bowl of chips.
3. Every 3 children will share a bowl of carrot sticks.
4. Every 6 children will share a bowl of popcorn.

How many children are coming to the party?

IMPOSSIBLE?

Which of these four shapes are real and which are impossible?

① ② ③ ④

SOLUTIONS

IMPOSSIBLE

Shapes 1 and 3 are real,
but shapes 2 and 4 are impossible.

A LOT OF FOOD

30

He is providing 30 bowls of pasta, 15 bowls of chips,
10 bowls of carrot sticks, 5 bowls of popcorn.

What is the next number in this sequence:

6421, 1246, 623, 326, 163?

NUMBERS 1 TO 9

Fill in the missing numbers so the sum is correct.
The digits 1 to 9 should appear only once.

		8	
1	2		
9		+	
4			

ON A TRAIN

The train from Aristoteltown to Platoville
goes exactly halfway, makes a stop at Philotown,
then travels 12 miles back the way it came.
It then powers toward Platoville, it spends 3 hours going the rest of
the way at 30 mph. How far is it from Aristoteltown to Platoville?
Finally, slowing its pace, for 1 mile.

SOLUTIONS

ON A TRAIN

158 miles
Half the distance is 79 miles:
90 miles (3 x 30 miles), minus 11 miles.

NUMBERS 1 TO 9

$$
\begin{array}{ccc}
 & \boxed{1} & \\
+\ \boxed{6} & \boxed{2} & \boxed{4} \\
\boxed{7} & \boxed{5} & \boxed{9} \\
\boxed{8} & \boxed{3} &
\end{array}
$$

SEQUENCE #8

361
The sequence is digits reversed, number halved, digits reversed, number halved.

NUMBER FUN

What number should replace the question mark?

7	9	2
3	?	5
10		

LETTER

Which letter of the Roman alphabet has been drawn here?

SOLUTIONS
- - - - - - - - - - -

LETTER
- -

E

NUMBER FUN

12

Add the 3 in the middle row to each top number
to find the number below it.

SEQUENCE #9

What is the next number in this sequence:

0, 1, 2, 10, 11, 12, 20, 21, 22?

PAINTING THE PALACE

Usually, 5 decorators repaint an area of the palace walls in 4 days. Each decorator covers 100 ft² per day. Unfortunately, 3 decorators are away. The remaining decorators have been asked to do the same job in 8 days. What area will each need to paint per day?

STAFFROOM

In the Jarndyce offices, half the staff are lawyers. One-fifth are accountants, while 25 are marketeers, while the administrative team is one-tenth of the size of the accountancy team. How many staff work for Jarndyce?

SOLUTIONS

STAFFROOM

100

We can use an equation where x is the total number of staff:

$\frac{1}{2}x + 25 + \frac{1}{5}x + \frac{1}{20}x = x$

$\frac{1}{4}x = 25, x = 100$

PAINTING THE PALACE

125 ft^2

The area to be painted is 2,000 ft^2 (5 x 4 x 100 ft^2 = 2,000 ft^2).
The remaining 2 painters take 8 days to do the work
(2,000 ft^2 ÷ 16 = 125 ft^2).

SEQUENCE #9

100

We are counting in the ternary (base 3) number system.

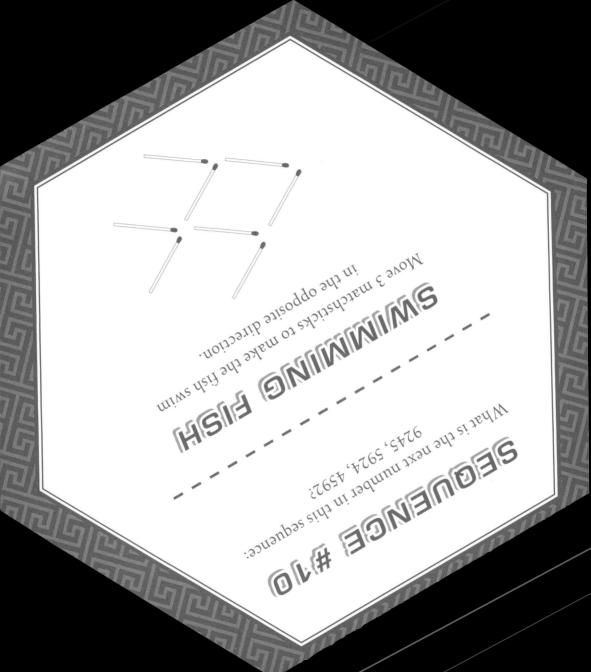

SWIMMING FISH

Move 3 matchsticks to make the fish swim in the opposite direction.

SEQUENCE #10

What is the next number in this sequence: 9245, 5924, 4592?

SOLUTIONS

SEQUENCE #10

2459

The last digit of the previous number always moves to the front.

SWIMMING FISH

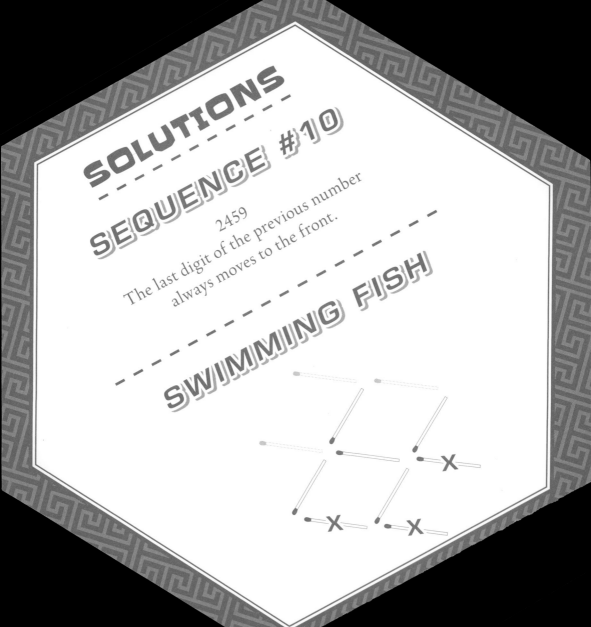

CHOCOLATE

When a mathematician is buying a box of chocolates, she notes that the cost of the chocolates is a rearrangement of the amount of money she has in her purse. Amusingly, the amount of money she has left after paying for the chocolates is a rearrangement of the three digits that make up the amount of money. How much do the chocolates cost?

SEQUENCE #11

What is the next number in this sequence:

3, 12, 6, 24, 12, 48?

SEQUENCE #12

What is the next number in this sequence:

220, 110, 0, 110, 110, 0, 110, -110?

SOLUTIONS

CHOCOLATE

$4.95 (or $4.59)

The mathematician started off with $9.54 in her purse. This answer is best arrived at by trial and error.

SEQUENCE #11

24

The sequence is x4, ÷2, x4, ÷2.

SEQUENCE #12

220

The sequence is
a – b = c, b – c = d, c – d = e.

EMPTY SEATS

At the end of a rock concert, 125 people are able to file out of the stadium every 3 minutes. If it takes 1 hour for the stadium to empty, how many people were at the concert?

SEQUENCE #13

What is the next number in this sequence: 3, 8, 23, 68?

SAFELY LOCKED

A mathematician has a new safe but can't remember the precise number needed to open it. However, she does remember that the number has 4 digits, all of which are different. It begins and ends with odd numbers, with two even numbers in the middle. She also remembers that it's divisible by 19 and 519. What number will open the safe?

SOLUTIONS

SAFELY LOCKED

9861

Simply, 19 x 519 = 9861

Another way to check this is by dividing 519 by 19, and continuing adding 519 to 519 and dividing by 19, and continuing in this way until you get this number.

SEQUENCE #13

203

The sequence is x3 – 1, x3 – 1.

EMPTY SEATS

2,500 people

If the time taken was 60 minutes, there were 20 batches of 125 people (1 batch every 3 minutes): 20 x 125 = 2,500.

ODD NUMBERS

If the sum of the first 50 odd numbers is 2,500, what is the sum of the first 75 odd numbers?

SHAPE SCRAPE

Which shape is next in the sequence:
A, B, C, or D?

SOLUTIONS

SHAPE SCRAPE

C

ODD NUMBERS

5,625

The sum of consecutive odd numbers starting with 1 is the number of odd numbers (in this case, 75) multiplied by itself: 75 x 75 = 5,625

STARS AND DIAMONDS

Reposition 6 matchsticks to make
6 equal diamonds:

SEQUENCE #14

What is the next number in this sequence:

1, 2, 5, 12, 27, 58, 121?

SEQUENCE #14

248

The sequence is $x2, x2 + 1, x2 + 2, x2 + 3,$
$x2 + 4, x2 + 5, x2 + 6.$

STARS AND DIAMONDS

SNACK TIME

At the movies, a group of friends buys popcorn. All except 1 snack each. All except 3 buy popcorn. All except 5 buy sweets. All except 4 buy ice cream. How many friends are there?

DRAWING CHALLENGE

Draw this shape without lifting your pencil and without going over the same line twice:

PAINTING

Jane can paint 1 of the rooms in the hotel in 4 hours, while Mary can paint a room in 2 hours. How long will it take them to paint a room if they work together?

SOLUTIONS

PAINTING

1 hour and 20 minutes

Mary's rate of work is twice Jane's,
so she will paint ⅔ of the room while Jane paints ⅓.
Mary can paint ⅔ of a room in 1 hour and 20 minutes.

DRAWING CHALLENGE

SNACK TIME

6 friends

17 A SIDE

Place the numbers 1 to 9 in the circles so that each side of the triangle adds up to 17.

TRIPLETS

By the time they are 1 year old, the Jones family triplets weigh quite different amounts. Bella weighs 2 lb more than Anna. The combined weight of Bella and Clara is 18 lb more than Anna. Clara weighs 2 lb more than Bella. What does Bella weigh?

SOLUTIONS

17 A SIDE

There is more than one possible solution, but here is an option:

TRIPLETS

14 lb. If each child's weight is represented by her initial:

$$A = B - 2$$
$$B + C = A + 18$$
$$C = B + 2$$

If the value of A from equation 1 is fed into equation 2:

$$B + C = B - 2 + 18$$
$$C = 16$$

If Clara weighs 16 lb, then Bella weighs 14 lb.

CHOCOLATE SQUARES

A chocolate bar is scored into 30 squares. You can break any existing piece of chocolate horizontally or vertically. How many times do you need to break the bar to make 10 pieces?

CUTTING A CLOVER

Making only two straight cuts, slice this four-leafed clover into as many pieces as possible. How many pieces can you make?

SEASHELLS

The seashell team picked up twice as many seashells on Tuesday afternoon as on Tuesday morning. On Wednesday, they picked up double the number they did they pick up on Tuesday afternoon? seashells they collected on Tuesday. If they picked up 99 in total, how many did they pick up on Tuesday afternoon?

SOLUTIONS

SEASHELLS

22

They picked up 11 on Tuesday morning, 22 on Tuesday afternoon and 66 on Wednesday.

CUTTING A CLOVER

6

CHOCOLATE SQUARES

9 times

You started with 1 piece and each break creates 1 more piece.

SPEEDING ALONG

The distance between Addville and Minusville is 220 miles. At the same moment, a car sets off from Addville, heading to the other town. They pass each other 2 hours later. If the motorbike sets off from Minusville, heading 10 mph faster than the car, what are their speeds?

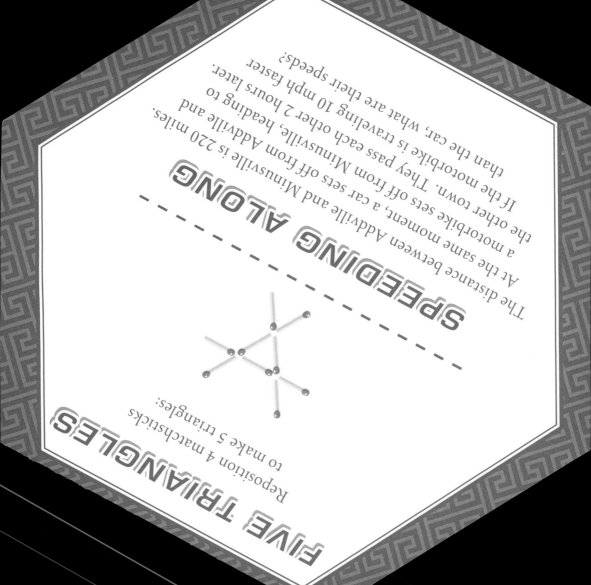

FIVE TRIANGLES

Reposition 4 matchsticks to make 5 triangles:

SPEEDING ALONG

The car was traveling at 50 mph and the
motorbike was traveling at 60 mph.
The distance traveled by the car in 2 hours
can be written as 2x (where x is its speed).
The distance traveled by the motorbike in 2 hours
can be written as 2(x + 10) or 2x + 20.
The 2 distances must add up to 220 miles, so:

$$2x + 2x + 20 = 220$$
$$x = 50$$

MATCHING PAIR

A mathematician needs to pack 1 pair of socks for an overnight trip. In her sock drawer, she has 11 pairs of blue socks, 3 pairs of green socks, and 13 pairs of yellow socks, all unmatched. She decides to choose her socks with her eyes closed. What is the lowest number of socks she must choose to be sure of having 1 matching pair?

RED SQUARES

A 4 in x 4 in cube is painted red on all 6 sides. It is then cut into equal 1 in x 1 in cubes. How many of these small cubes will have red paint on 3 sides, on 2 sides, on 1 side, or on no sides?

SOLUTIONS

MATCHING PAIR

4

Since there are 3 different colors of sock in her drawer, if she takes 4 socks, at least 2 of them will match.

RED SQUARES

8 cubes have red paint on 3 sides, 24 have paint on 2 sides, 24 have paint on 1 side, and 8 have no paint at all. There are 64 cubes in total.

ON TIME

Doctor Tangent is driving to a conference. Three hours after leaving home, she notices that she will be 20 minutes late, unless she increases her speed, and that, unless she increases her speed by 10 mph, she has driven 150 miles and that, and arrives on time. What distance is it from her home to the conference?

SOLUTIONS
ON TIME

250 miles

This can be worked out with equations, where T is the time (in hours) taken to complete the journey and x is the distance remaining to be traveled when Tangent checks her progress.

The equation for the journey completed on time:

$$T = 3 + x/60$$

The equation for the journey if Tangent does not speed up:

$$T + \frac{1}{3} = 3 + x/50 \text{ (or } T = 2\frac{2}{3} + x/50)$$

Put this value for T into the first equation and then simplify:

$$2\frac{2}{3} + x/50 = 3 + x/60$$
$$x/50 - x/60 = \frac{1}{3}$$
$$x = 100$$

SEQUENCE #15

What is the next number in this sequence:

1, 1, 2, 6, 24, 120?

NEXT?

Which shape comes next in the sequence: A, B, C, D, E, or F?

?

SEQUENCE #15

720

The sequence is x1, x2, x3, x4, x5, x6.

NEXT?

C

FIGURE IT OUT

What number should replace the question mark?

- - - - - - - - - -

MARBLE MANIA

Al, Bea, and Clive play a game of marbles. Each starts with 20 marbles. In the first round, Al wins 6 marbles from Clive, but loses 5 to Clive, while Bea wins 2 from Al and 3 from Clive. In the second round, Bea wins 2 from Al and 6 from Clive, but Clive wins 4 from Al. In the third round, Clive wins 6 from Bea, but Bea wins 2 from Al. Who has the most marbles?

SOLUTIONS

FIGURE IT OUT

16

In each set of triangles, the top right number is the product of the 2 other numbers.

MARBLE MANIA

Clive

Clive has 36, Al has 7 and Bea has 17.

JOGGING ROUTE

A jogger always runs the same route at a steady speed of 6 mph. One day, she speeds up by 2 mph and finishes the route 10 minutes quicker than usual. How long is her route?

WHAT'S IN THE BAG?

In bag one are 3 red balls and 5 blue balls. In bag two are 8 blue balls. Randomly choose 2 balls from bag one. If the balls are the same color, put them to one side and put a blue ball from bag two into bag one. If the chosen balls are different colors, put the blue ball aside and put the red ball back from bag one. Continue choosing from bag one in the same way, until there is one ball left in bag one. What color is the last ball in bag one?

SOLUTIONS

JOGGING ROUTE

4 miles

This could be worked out with a pair of equations,
where x is the distance and T is the time in hours:

At the usual running speed: $x/6 = T$

At the faster running speed: $x/8 = T - 1/6$

Put the value for T from equation 1 into equation 2 and simplify:

$$x/8 = x/6 - 1/6$$
$$6x = 8x - 8$$
$$2x = 8$$
$$x = 4$$

WHAT'S IN THE BAG

Red

Since you started with an odd number of red balls
and can only remove pairs, you will always have
to replace the last red ball in bag one.

YOGURTS

A large box holds 12 yogurts, a medium box holds 6 yogurts and a small box holds 3. A yogurt packer has 5 large boxes, 10 medium boxes, and 20 small boxes. A customer has asked that at least 2 boxes in their order are small-sized. What is the smallest number of boxes that the packer can use for 111 yogurts, ensuring that no boxes have empty space?

- - - - - - - - - - -

DIAMONDS

Reposition 6 matchsticks to make 6 equal diamonds:

SOLUTIONS

YOGURTS

15 boxes

9 yogurts go in 3 small boxes, 60 yogurts go in 5 large boxes, 42 yogurts go in 7 medium boxes.

DIAMONDS

ON A KEYRING

Find two identical keys:

BARTER FOR FRUIT

At the market in Mathton, all trade is done by barter. How many apples would be needed to buy a bunch of grapes?

SOLUTIONS

ON A KEYRING

2 and 12

BARTER FOR FRUIT

10 apples

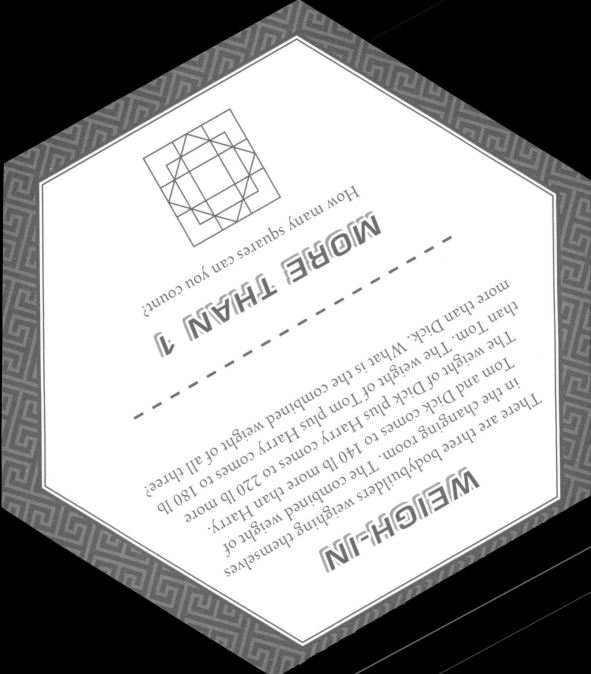

How many squares can you count?

WEIGH-IN

There are three bodybuilders weighing themselves in the changing room. The combined weight of Tom and Dick comes to 140 lb more than Harry. The combined weight of Dick plus Harry comes to 220 lb more than Tom. The weight of Dick plus Tom plus Harry comes to 180 lb more than Tom. What is the combined weight of all three?

WEIGH-IN

540 lb

This can be worked out with a series of equations, where each man's weight is represented by his initial:

$$T + D = H + 140$$
$$D + H = T + 220$$
$$T + H = D + 180$$

Using equation 3, we can say: $D = T + H - 180$
By substituting that into equation 1, we get:

$$T + T + H - 90 = H + 140$$
$$2T = 320$$
$$T = 160$$

It is then straightforward to work out that Dick weighs 180 lb and Harry weighs 200 lb.

MORE THAN 1

DO THE MATH

Replace the ?s with operators (+ − × ÷)
so that the following equation is true
(you may also use brackets if you like):

2 ? 4 ? 6 ? 8 = 10

GEARING UP

Gear 1 rotates anticlockwise. A and B are
crossed belt drives. Which directions do
gears 2, 3, 4, 5, 6, 7, and 8 rotate?

GEARING UP

2, 3, 4, 6, and 7 rotate clockwise,
but gears 5 and 8 rotate counterclockwise.

DO THE MATH

$(2 \times 4) - 6 + 8 = 10$

(The brackets are not strictly necessary.)

SEQUENCE #16

What is the next number in this sequence:

12, 17, 29, 46, 75, 121?

GAME OF CUPS

A woman is playing a traditional game of cups at the fairground; a ball is placed under one of three cups then the cups are switched with each other. To start the game, the showman places the ball under the left cup. In the first switch, the left cup is switched with another cup. In the second switch, the left cup is switched with another cup. In the third switch, the left cup is not moved. Which cup is most likely to be covering the ball?

SOLUTIONS

GAME OF CUPS

The left cup

There is a 50 percent chance the ball is under the left cup, but only a 25 percent that each of the other two cups is covering it.

SEQUENCE #16

196

The sequence is

$a + b = c, b + c = d, c + d = e.$

CROSSING THE RIVER

A mother, father, son, and daughter need to cross a river. They find an abandoned boat, which will take the weight of only one adult or two children at once. How many times does the boat have to cross the river to deliver the whole family to the other side?

CURLY SUE

Match up the pairs of identical curls.

SOLUTIONS

CURLY SUE

1 and 4, 2 and 3, 5 and 12, 6 and 11, 8 and 9, 7 and 10

9 times.

CROSSING THE RIVER

On crossing 1, the son and daughter travel to the other side. On crossing 2, the daughter returns with the boat. On crossing 3, the father travels to the other side. On crossing 4, the son returns with the boat. On crossing 5, the son and daughter travel to the other side. On crossing 6, the daughter returns with the boat. On crossing 7, the mother travels to the other side. On crossing 8, the son returns with the boat. On crossing 9, the son and daughter travel to the other side.

- - - - - - - - - - - - -

The train track between Alton Station and Balton Station is 300 miles. At 9 a.m., the express train sets off from Alton and the slow train sets off from Balton, heading to the other station. After 1.5 hours, the slow train makes a 1-hour stop. If the express is traveling 20 mph faster than the slow train (ignoring any stops), what are their speeds?

INHERITANCE

A mother wants to divide her land equally between four daughters, so that each child's land is an equal area, the same shape, contains one wind turbine and has access to the well.

SOLUTIONS

INHERITANCE

CATCHING THE TRAIN

The slow train is traveling at 48 mph, while the express train is traveling at 68 mph.

After 3 hours, the slow train has been moving for only 2 hours. The distance it has covered can be written as 2x (where x is its speed). The distance covered by the express can be written as 3(x + 20) or 3x + 60.

The 2 distances must add up to 300 miles so we can say:

$$2x + 3x + 60 = 300$$
$$x = 48$$

A HUNGRY LION

A woman is trapped in a room with two possible exit doors. Through door one is a corridor made of magnifying glass, through which the blazing sun fries to a crisp anyone who enters. Through door two is a hungry lion. How does the woman escape?

DOTS AND SPOTS

Which rectangle fills the blank space: A, B, or C?

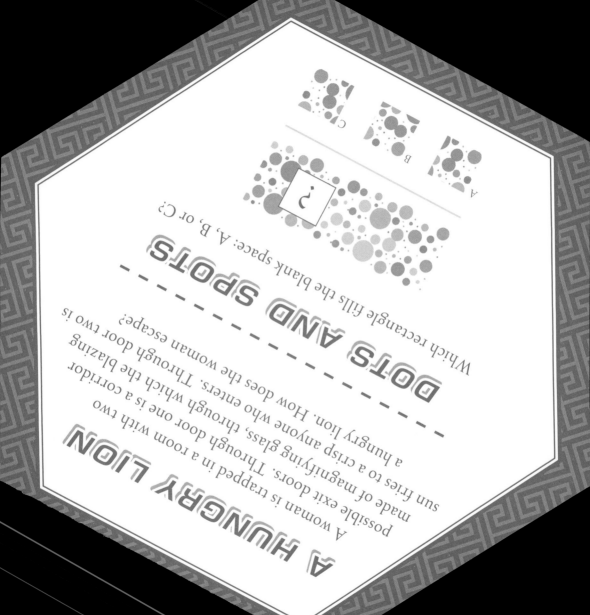

SOLUTIONS

HUNGRY LION

She waits until the sun sets, then takes door one.

DOTS AND SPOTS

A

ODD ONE OUT

You have nine identical-looking balls, but one of the balls is heavier than the others. You may put some or all of the balls on a traditional balance weighing scale to discover which ball is heavier. You may only use the scale twice. How do you do it?

SEQUENCE #17

What is the next number in this sequence:
1, 3, 15, 255, 65535?

SOLUTIONS

- - - - - - - - - -

ODD ONE OUT

Weigh any 3 balls against another 3 balls to discover which group of 3 contains the heavier ball. From that group of 3, weigh any 2 balls against each other.

- - - - - - - - - -

SEQUENCE #17

4294967295

The sequence is 1, 1(1 + 2) = 3,
3(3 + 2) = 15, 15(15 +2) = 255,
255(255 +2) = 65535,
65535(65535 + 2) = 4294967295

FIND A NUMBER

What number should replace the question mark?

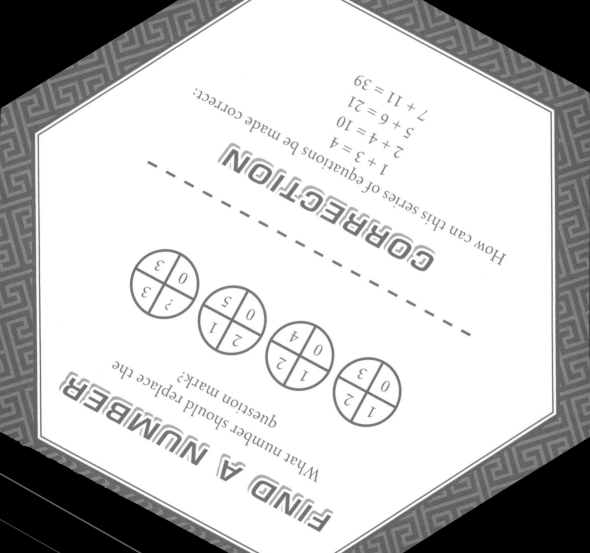

- - - - - - - - - - - - - - - - - -

CORRECTION

How can this series of equations be made correct:

$$1 + 3 = 4$$
$$2 + 4 = 10$$
$$5 + 6 = 21$$
$$7 + 11 = 39$$

SOLUTIONS

FIND A NUMBER

3

Moving from left to right, the sum of the numbers in each circle is 6, 7, 8, and 9.

CORRECTION

Add the last number of the previous line to the current line.

$1 + 3 = 4$

$4 + 2 + 4 = 10$

$10 + 5 + 6 = 21$

$21 + 7 + 11 = 39$

BACTERIA

A biologist places a single bacterium in a Petri dish at 9 a.m. At 9.01 a.m., the bacterium divides in two. At 9.02 a.m., each bacterium divides again. The bacteria continue dividing at the same rate until, at 10.14 a.m., the Petri dish is half full. At what time will it be full?

- - - - - - - - - -

CIRCLING

Which shape is next in the sequence: A, B, or C?

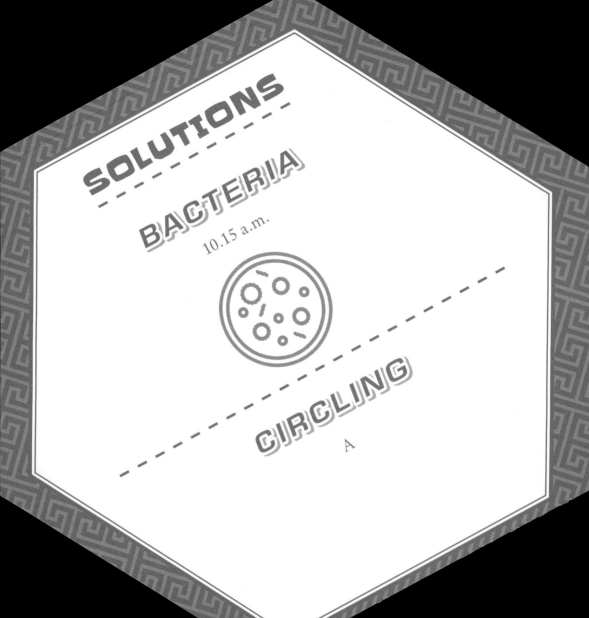

SOLUTIONS

BACTERIA

10.15 a.m.

CIRCLING

A

MISSING NUMBERS

In this sequence puzzle, the relationship between the first 2 numbers in each row is always the same, while the relationship between the last 2 numbers is always the same but different from the first relationship. What are the missing numbers?

1 2 1
2 6 3
7 56 28
? ? 66

CHEESE CUTTER

Cut this piece of cheese into two pieces so that it will fit into the box:

CHEESE
10 cm
3 cm

BOX
15 cm
2 cm

SOLUTIONS

CHEESE CUTTER

5 cm
1 cm
10 cm
2 cm

MISSING NUMBERS

11 132

The first relationship is $a(a + 1) = b$, while the second relationship is $b \div 2 = c$.

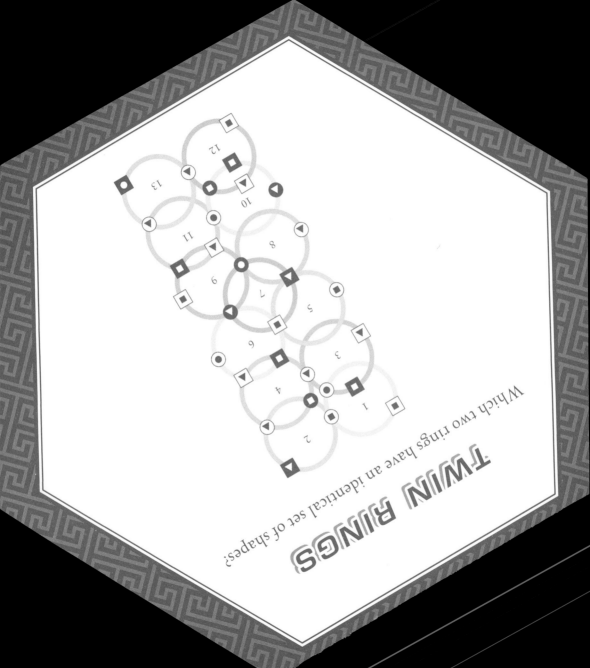

TWIN RINGS

Which two rings have an identical set of shapes?

WORK IT OUT

At the crochet club, two crocheters are working on an order from a tablecloth company. If John worked alone, he could complete the order in 10 days, while Mary could only complete half of the order in that time. Mary works alone for a while, then John joins her, so they complete the order together in 8 days. How many days did John work?

What number should replace the question mark?

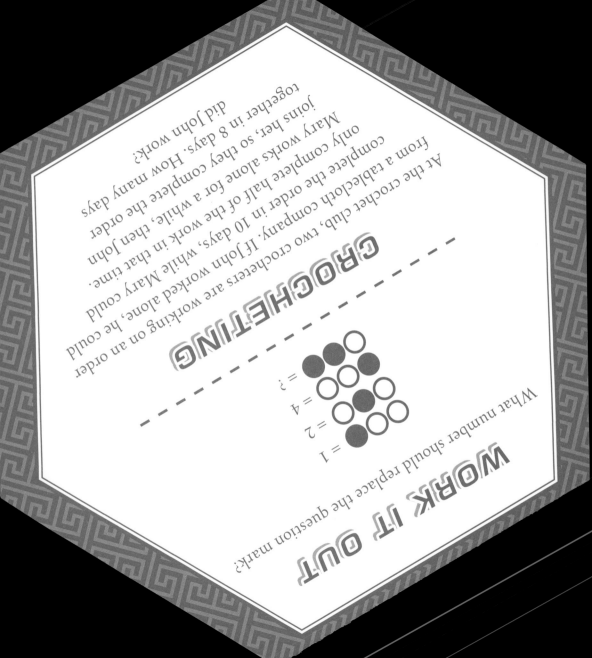

= 1

= 2

= 4

= ?

SOLUTIONS

WORK IT OUT

3

We are working in the binary system, where

○ = 0 and ● = 1

6 days

CROCHETING

John's work rate is 1/10 of the order per day, while Mary's is 1/20. Working for 8 days, Mary completes 8/20 of the work, or 4/10, which means that John must complete the remaining 6/10, so he works for 6 days.

AT THE BRIDGE

On a moonless night, four hikers arrive at a bridge that will take the weight of only two people at once. The bridge must be crossed using a torch, but the group shares only one torch. Hiker A can cross the bridge in 1 minute, hiker B in 2 minutes, hiker C in 5 minutes, and hiker D in 10 minutes. If hikers walk together, they must keep to the pace of the slower walker. What is the shortest time in which all 4 hikers can cross the bridge?

SOLVE THE PROBLEM!

- - - - - - - - -

What number should replace the question mark?

SOLUTIONS
- - - - - - - -
AT THE BRIDGE

17 minutes

Hikers A and B cross together, taking 2 minutes.

Hiker A returns with the torch, taking 1 minute.

Hikers C and D cross together, taking 10 minutes.

Hiker B returns with the torch, taking 2 minutes.

Hikers A and B cross together, taking 2 minutes.

- - - - - - - -
SOLVE THE PROBLEM

4

In each square, the bottom number divided by the top number is the same as the right number divided by the left number.

COMBINATION

Which shape combines 1 and 2: A, B, or C?

1

2

?

A

B

C

DOGGY RACE

There are three dogs are competing in a 100 ft race. Rover runs at an average speed of 10 ft/sec, but after 80 ft rests for 5 seconds, before running at the same speed as before. Bella runs at 16 ft/sec, but stops after 6 seconds for a 3-second scratch, then continues at the same speed. Charlie has a speed of 12 ft/sec. Which dog crosses the finish line first?

SOLUTIONS

COMBINATION

C

DOGGY RACE

Rover.

Rover finishes in 10 seconds. Bella runs 72 ft in the first 6 seconds, stops for 3 seconds, then completes the last 28 ft in 21/3 seconds, giving her a total time of roughly 111/3 seconds (we do not know how fast she accelerates, but we know enough to judge she must be slightly behind Rover).

Charlie completes the first 80 ft in 5 seconds, then rests for 5 seconds, so he is still resting when Rover passes the finish line.

ON THE FARM!

Tillie and Billie are ploughing their land with two tractors. If Tillie did all the ploughing alone, she would finish in 8 days. Billie would complete it alone in 10 days. At first, Billie works alone, then Tillie joins her, so they finish together in 5 days. How many days did Tillie work?

SEQUENCE #18

What is the next number in this sequence:

2, 6, 3, 12, 4, 18, 5, 24, 6?

SOLUTIONS

ON THE FARM

4 days

Tillie's rate of work is ⅛ of the land per day (or 10/80). Billie's rate of work is 1/10 (or 8/80). Billie works for 5 days, so she ploughs 40/80 of the land. The remaining 40/80 must be done by Tillie, so she works for 4 days.

SEQUENCE #18

30

There are 2 sequences, running alternately: 2, 3, 4, 5, 6... and 6, 12, 18, 24, 30.

Which shape is next in the sequence: A, B, or C?

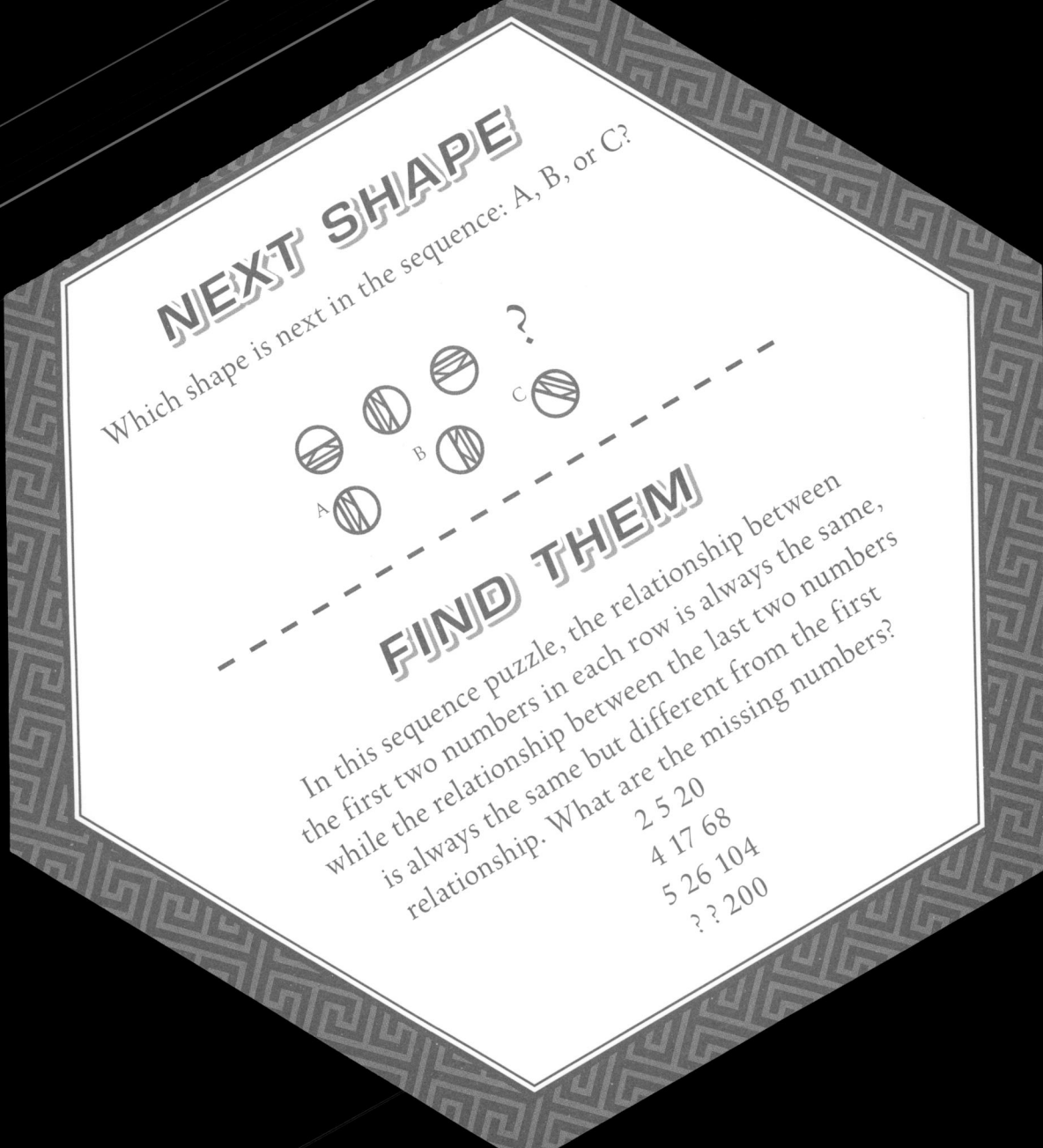

FIND THEM

In this sequence puzzle, the relationship between the first two numbers in each row is always the same, while the relationship between the last two numbers is always the same but different from the first relationship. What are the missing numbers?

2 5 20
4 17 68
5 26 104
? ? 200

SOLUTIONS

NEXT SHAPE

B

FIND THEM

7 50

The first relationship is $a^2 + 1 = b$, while the second relationship is $b \times 4 = c$.

SPADES AND CLUBS

How many cards would you need to draw
from a deck of 52 playing cards to be sure
of getting a black queen?

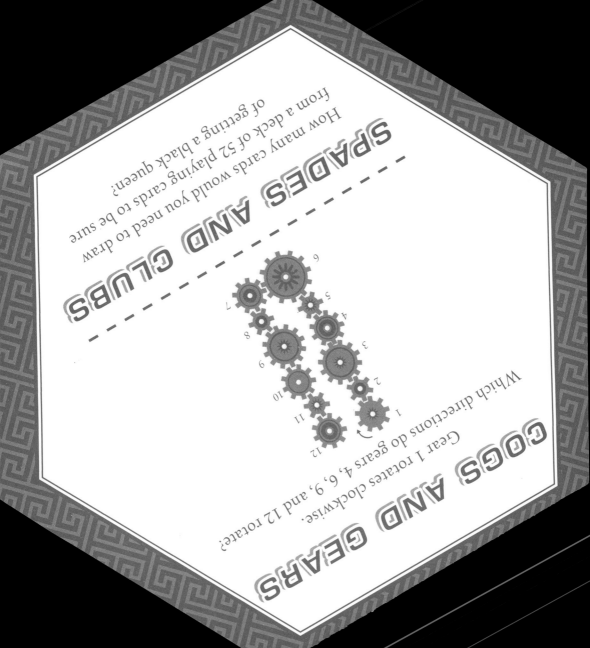

COGS AND GEARS

Which directions do gears 4, 6, 9, and 12 rotate?
Gear 1 rotates clockwise.

SOLUTIONS

COGS AND GEARS

Gears 4, 6, and 12 rotate counterclockwise, but gear 9 rotates clockwise.

SPADES AND CLUBS

51

The two black queens may be cards 51 and 52.

7 TRIANGLES

Reposition 2 matchsticks to make 7 triangles:

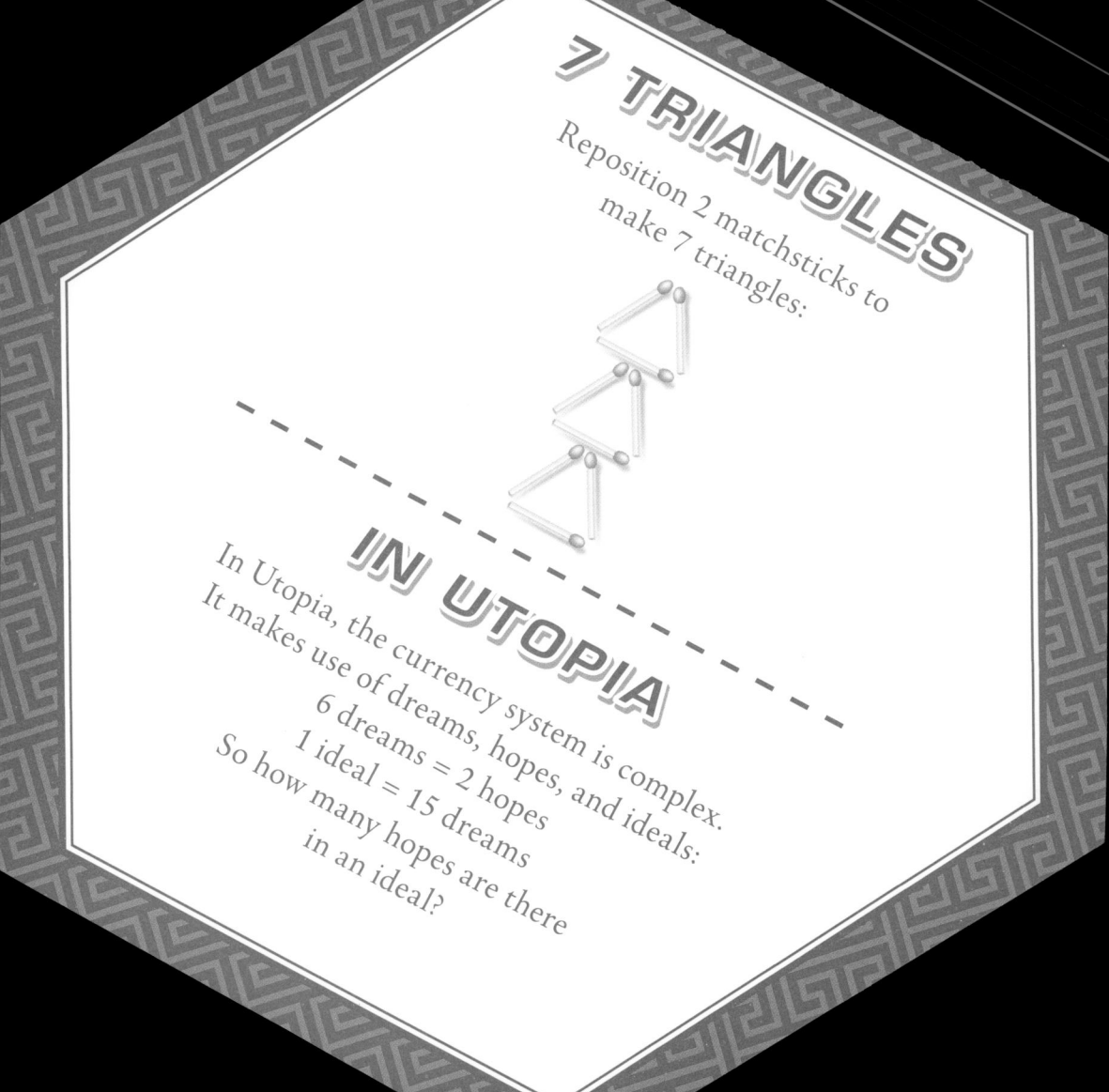

IN UTOPIA

In Utopia, the currency system is complex.
It makes use of dreams, hopes, and ideals:
6 dreams = 2 hopes
1 ideal = 15 dreams
So how many hopes are there
in an ideal?

7 TRIANGLES

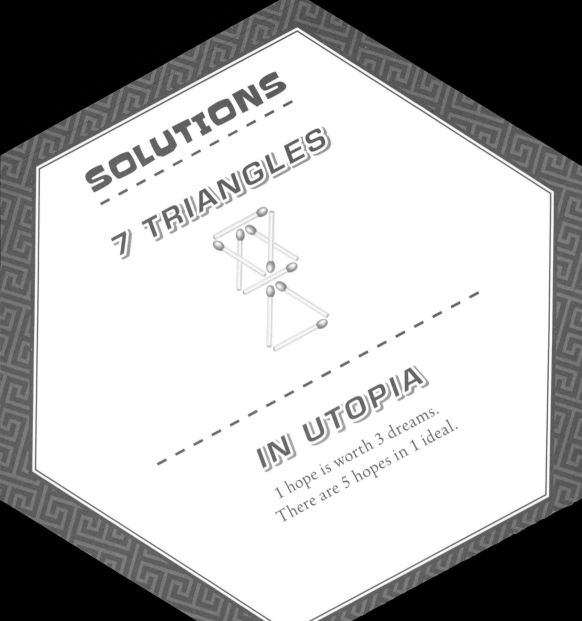

IN UTOPIA

1 hope is worth 3 dreams.
There are 5 hopes in 1 ideal.

LIGHT UP

There are three light switches in the hallway, each of which turns on one of three light bulbs in the cellar. You want to descend into the dusty cellar only once, so how can you discover which switch operates which light bulb?

NUMBER SUM

What numbers should replace the question marks?

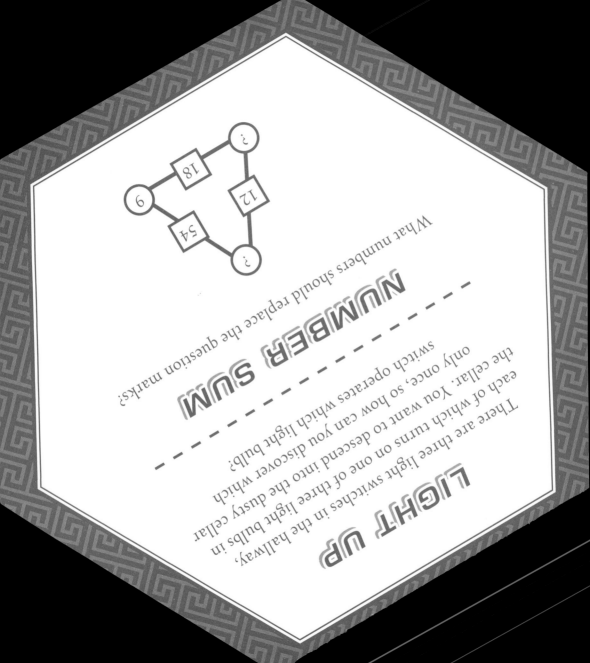

SOLUTIONS

LIGHT UP

Turn on one switch for long enough to warm its bulb, then turn it off. Turn on one other switch, then descend immediately to the cellar. You will find one warm bulb, one lit bulb, and one off bulb.

NUMBER SUM

The numbers in the squares are the product of the numbers on either side.

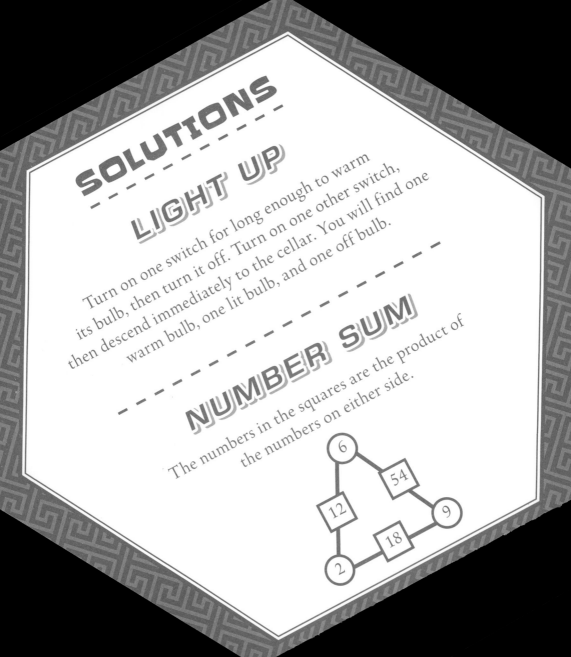

CLASSIC PARTY

A classicist is organizing a party for Greek and Latin scholars, who are either orange juice or lemonade for each of the scholars. She will provide either orange juice or lemonade for all her invitees, who are either Hellenists or Latinists or Latinists. She asks down these facts which they would drink Hellenists or Latinists. She asks 8 invitees which she is inviting 8 Hellenists; Latinists who prefer orange juice; 7 of the invitees are Hellenists who prefer lemonade; 4 of the friends prefer orange juice. How many friends is the classicist inviting?

A   B   C

Which shape completes the cube: A, B, or C?

COMPLETE

SOLUTIONS

COMPLETE

C

CLASSIC PARTY

19 friends
There are 8 Hellenists (4 prefer orange juice and 4 prefer lemonade) and 11 Latinists (4 prefer orange juice and 7 lemonade).

FISHES

An aquarium contains an equal number of hairy frogfish and warty frogfish. A hairy frogfish eats 3 shrimps and 2 crabs per day. A warty frogfish eats 4 shrimps and 1 crab per day. If 21 shrimps and 9 crabs are eaten in one day, how many hairy frogfish and warty frogfish are there?

- - - - - - - - -

MOVE IT!

Reposition 4 matchsticks to make 3 equal triangles:

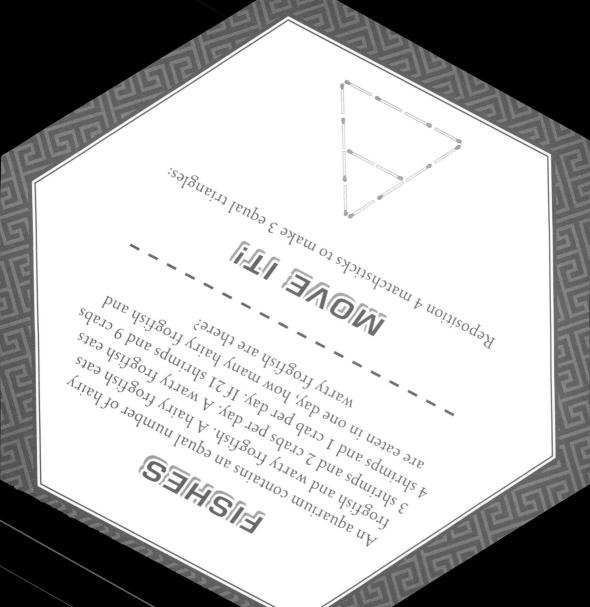

SOLUTIONS

FISHES

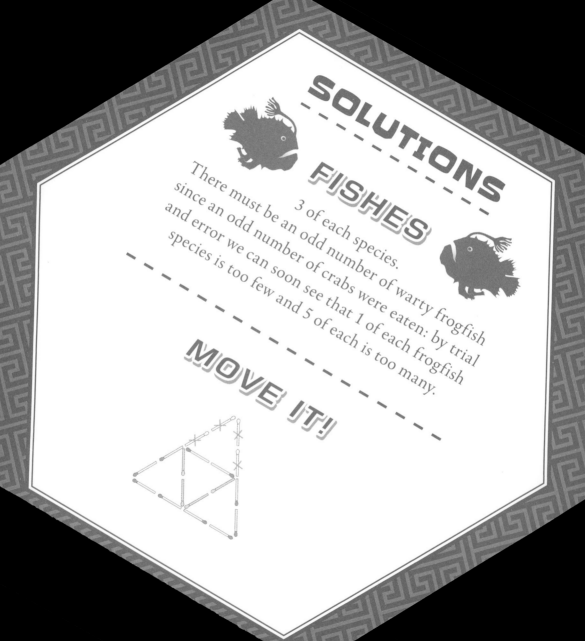

3 of each species. There must be an odd number since an odd number of warty frogfish were eaten: by trial and error we can soon see that 1 of each frogfish species is too few and 5 of each is too many.

MOVE IT!

TEA TIME!

Find the overhead view for each teapot:

GET TO 1,000

How can eight 8s equal 1,000?

SOLUTIONS

TEA TIME

2:5, 4:9, 6:7, 8:1, 10:3, 12:11

GET TO 1,000

$(8888 - 888) \div 8 = 1,000$

FAMILY TREE

A boy has as many sisters as brothers, but each sister has half as many brothers and sisters are in the family?

How many brothers and sisters are in the family?

ROLL IT OUT

Which shape is next in the sequence: A, B, or C?

SOLUTIONS

ROLL IT OUT

B

FAMILY TREE

4 brothers and 3 sisters

CUBISM!

Which cube is identical to the one above:
A, B, C, or D?

THE RIGHT SET

Find a set of three whole numbers whose
product is equal to their sum.

CUBISM

C

THE RIGHT SET

$1 + 2 + 3 = 1 \times 2 \times 3$

Match the shapes to make 7 circles:

SEVEN CIRCLES

How can six 3s equal 369?

369

SOLUTIONS

369

333 + 33 + 3 = 369

SEVEN CIRCLES

1:10, 2:9, 3:14, 4:8, 5:11, 6:12, 7:13

LUNCH TIME

The schoolchildren are already hungry for their lunch, which is served at 1 p.m. Their teacher tells them that if it were 3 hours later, it would be half as long until lunch as it would be if it were 2 hours later. What time is it now?

- - - - - - - -

CYCLE RACE

The annual cycle race is 300 miles. Unusually, there are only 2 competitors, who start from opposite ends of the course. One of them races 10 mph/h faster than the other. Find the speed of both cyclists if, after 2 hours, there are 44 miles between them.

SOLUTIONS

CYCLE RACE

Cyclist 1 races at 27 mph, while cyclist 2 races at 37 mph. This can be worked out with an equation where the speed of the slower cyclist is x and the speed of the faster is x + 10. The distance covered in 4 hours by the second is 4(x + 10) while the distance covered by the first is 4x:

$$4(x + 10) + 4x = 300 - 44$$
$$4x + 40 + 4x = 256$$
$$8x = 216$$
$$x = 27$$

LUNCH TIME

9 a.m.

THE JONESES

Mr. and Mrs. Jones have 7 daughters and each daughter has 2 brothers. How many people are in the immediate family?

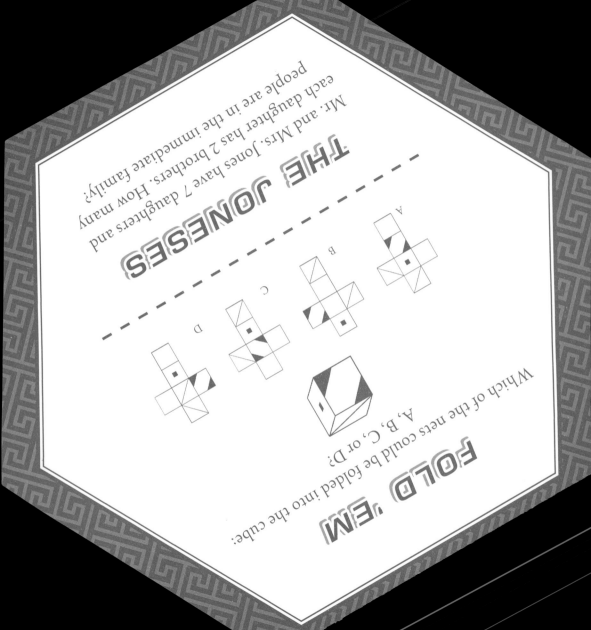

FOLD 'EM

Which of the nets could be folded into the cube: A, B, C, or D?

A

B

C

D

SOLUTIONS

FOLD 'EM

C

THE JONESES

11

There are 2 parents, 7 daughters, and 2 brothers.

FOUNTAINS

In the palace courtyard, 2 fountains are in front of 2 fountains, 2 fountains are behind 2 fountains, and 2 fountains are beside 2 fountains. How many fountains are there?

SOLVE IT

In this sequence puzzle, the relationship between the first two numbers in each row is always the same, while the relationship between the last two numbers is always the same but different from the first relationship. What are the missing numbers?

2 6 12
3 9 15
4 12 18
? ? 39

SOLUTIONS

SOLVE IT

11 33

The first relationship is a x 3 = b, while the second relationship is b + 6 = c.

FOUNTAINS

4

They are in a square.

HOW OLD IS HE?

Today, Herman's age is 4 times his son's age, but only 5 years ago, his age was 7 times his son's. How old will Herman be in 10 years?

SHAPE UP

What number should replace the question mark?

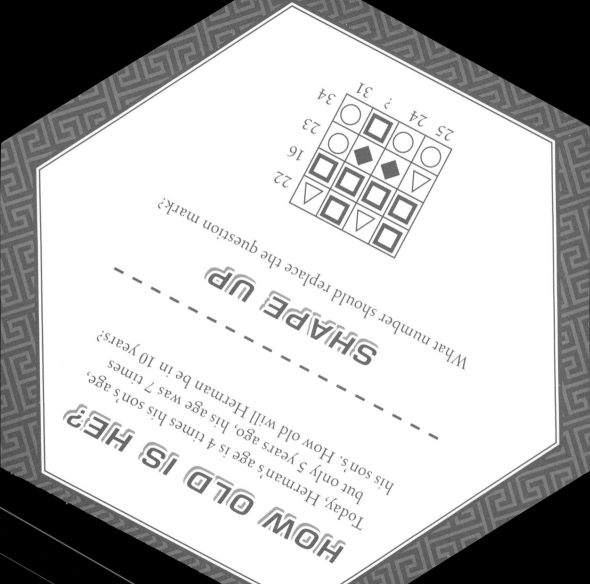

25 24 ? 31
23
34
16
22

SOLUTIONS

HOW OLD IS HE?

50

Today, Herman is 40 and his son is 10, while 5 years ago he was 35 and his son was 5.

SHAPE UP

15

□ = 4

△ = 7

◆ = 3

○ = 10

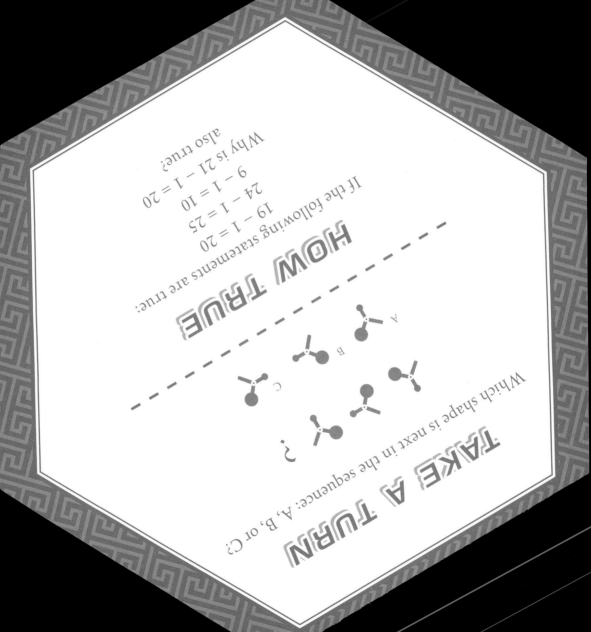

TAKE A TURN

Which shape is next in the sequence: A, b, or C?

A
b
C
?

HOW TRUE

If the following statements are true:

19 − 1 = 20
24 − 1 = 25
9 − 1 = 10

Why is 21 − 1 = 20 also true?

SOLUTIONS

TAKE A TURN

C

HOW TRUE

We are working with Roman numerals, so:

Remove I from IXX and we get XX

Remove I from XXIV and we get XXV

Remove I from IX and we get X

But when we remove I from XXI we get XX

DECK OF CARDS

How many cards would you need to draw
from a deck of 52 playing cards to be sure of
getting cards from more than 1 suit?

- - - - - - - - - - - - - - - - - -

COUNT THE SHAPES

Count the number of squares, rectangles,
triangles, circles, and pentagons:

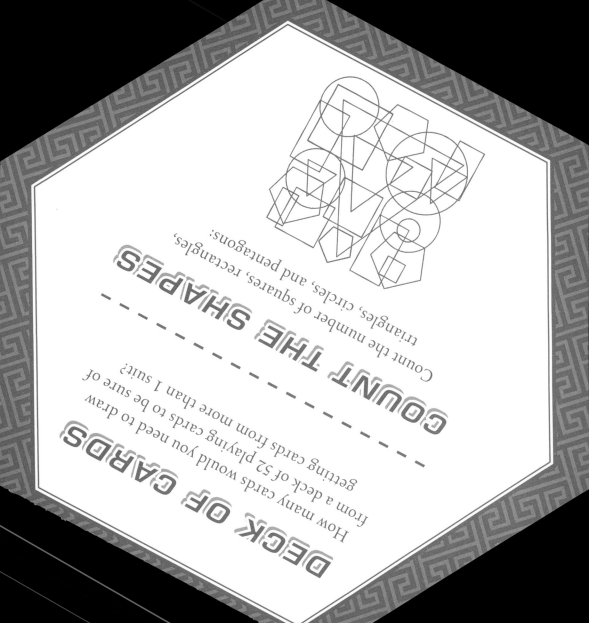

SOLUTIONS

DECK OF CARDS

14

Since there are 13 cards in each suit, you would need to draw 14 cards, just in case all 13 of your first cards were from the same suit.

COUNT THE SHAPES

5 squares, 7 rectangles, 14 triangles, 5 circles, and 4 pentagons

TRIANGULATION

What number should replace the question mark?

PLANT TREES

During a reforestation project, each girl in the group plants 3 rowans, while each boy plants 1 silver birch. There are an equal number of boys and girls. After two days, 48 trees have been planted. How many rowans and birches have been planted?

SOLUTIONS

PLANT TREES

36 rowans and 12 silver birches.
The trees must be split in the ratio 3:1,
so ¾ of the trees are rowans.

TRIANGULATION

22
In each triangle, the bottom number is
twice the sum of the top 2 numbers.

IN THE MUSEUM

A mathematician went to the archaeology museum. She spent one-sixth of her time in the Egyptology rooms. She took a break for 1 hour to have lunch. After that, she spent one-third of her total time looking at Roman artifacts. She then spent twice as long in the Indus Valley rooms as she had in the Egyptology rooms. How long did she spend at the museum?

PEN TO PAPER

Draw this shape without lifting your pencil and without going over the same line twice:

SOLUTIONS

PEN TO PAPER

IN THE MUSEUM

6 hours

We can write an equation where x is the total time in the museum:

$$\tfrac{1}{6}x + 1 + \tfrac{1}{3}x + \tfrac{2}{6}x = x$$

$$\tfrac{1}{6}x = 1$$

$$x = 6$$

GRANDMA'S AGE

When Olivia asked her Grandma how old she was, she was given the following answer: "I have had 6 children and there are 4 years between each one. I had my first child when I was 19, and now the youngest is 19."
How old is Olivia's Grandma?

- - - - - - - - - - - -

HEXAGONS

Which of the hexagons will fill the empty triangles in the template: A, B, C, D, E, or F?

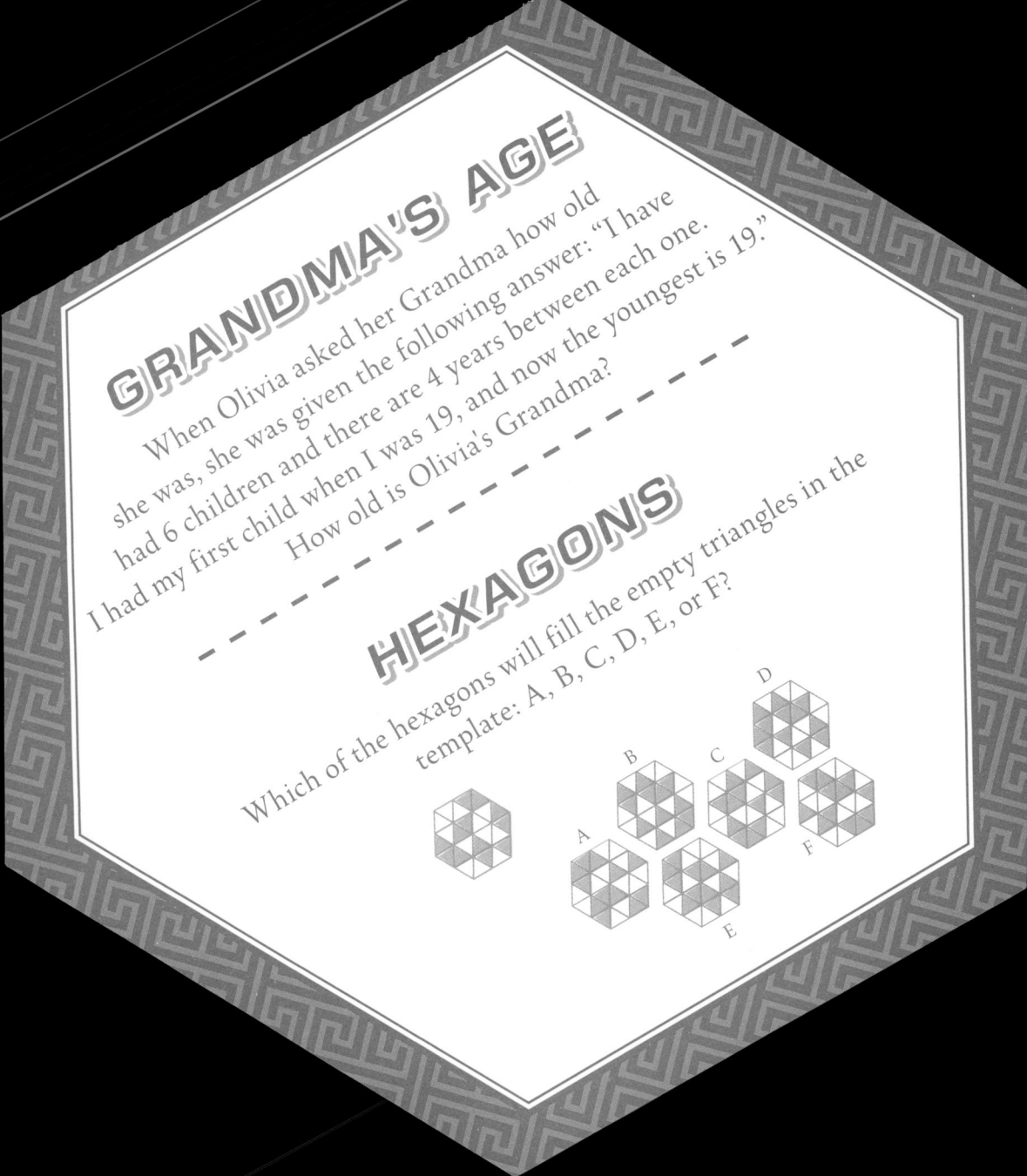

SOLUTIONS

GRANDMA'S AGE

58

Grandma was 19 when she had her first child, 23 when she had her second, 27 when she had her third, 31 when she had her fourth, 35 when she had her fifth, and 39 when she had her sixth, who is now 19.

19 + 4 + 4 + 4 + 4 + 4 + 19 = 58

HEXAGONS

C

IT'S TRUE

How could this equation be true?

8 + 8 = 91

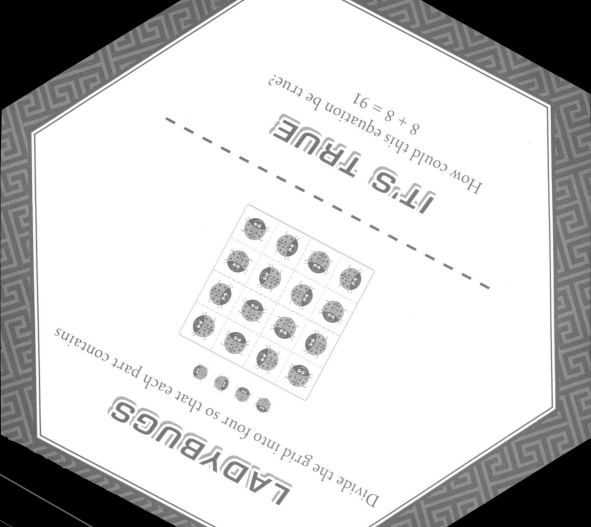

LADYBUGS

Divide the grid into four so that each part contains

LADYBUGS

IT'S TRUE

It is correct when it is turned
upside down: 16 = 8 + 8.

FIVE-DIGIT NUMBER

Find a 5-digit number for which the following statement is true: "If 1 is placed as an additional digit at the end, then the number becomes three times bigger than if 1 was placed at the beginning."

HEAD OVER HEELS

What is the smallest number that increases by 12 when it is turned upside down?

A LONG JOB

For a tiler to complete the office floor in time, she must lay 12 ft² per day. However, she is only able to lay 8 ft² per day, so the job takes 4 days longer than planned. How long should the work have taken?

SOLUTIONS

A LONG JOB

8 days

The solution can be found using an equation where
x is the planned time:

$$12x = 8(x + 4)$$
$$4x = 32$$
$$x = 8$$

HEAD OVER HEELS

86

When turned upside down, it is 98.

FIVE-DIGIT NUMBER

42857

$$428571 = 3 \times 142857$$

MAKE A CUBE

Which cube can be made with this net:
A, B, C, D, or E?

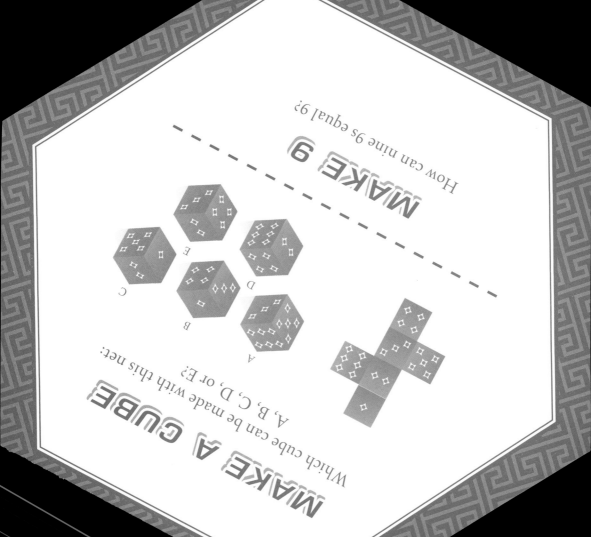

MAKE 9

How can nine 9s equal 9?

MAKE A CUBE

C

MAKE 9

$999 - 999 + 9 + 9 - 9 = 9$

HEART TO HEART

How many cards would you need to draw from a deck of 52 playing cards to be sure of getting the complete suit of hearts?

- - - - - - - - - -

DIVIDE THE GRID

Divide the grid into four so that each part contains

SOLUTIONS

HEART TO HEART

52

The last heart may be the very last card in the pack.

DIVIDE THE GRID

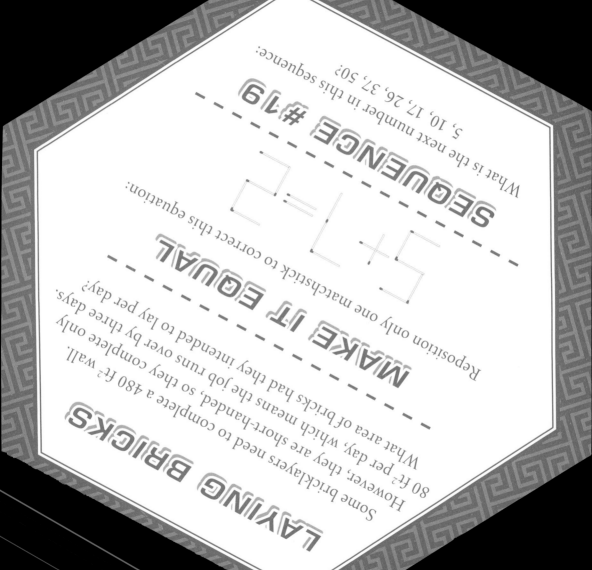

LAYING BRICKS

Some bricklayers need to complete a 480 ft² wall. However, they are short-handed, so they complete only 80 ft² per day, which means the job runs over by three days. What area of bricks had they intended to lay per day?

MAKE IT EQUAL

Reposition only one matchstick to correct this equation:

$$5+7=2$$

SEQUENCE #19

What is the next number in this sequence:

5, 10, 17, 26, 37, 50?

SOLUTIONS

LAYING BRICKS

160 ft²

They spend 6 days doing the work rather than the planned 3 days: 480 ÷ 3 = 160.

MAKE IT EQUAL

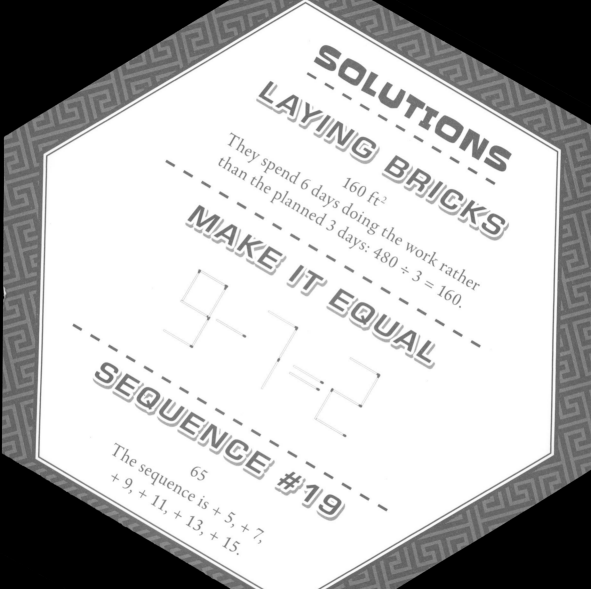

SEQUENCE #19

65

The sequence is + 5, + 7, + 9, + 11, + 13, + 15.

TAKE YOUR PICK

Which shape combines 1 and 2: A, B, or C?

1

2

?

A

B

C

TEN-DIGIT NUMBER

Find a 10-digit number where the first digit is how many 0s are in the number, the second digit is how many 1s are in the number, and so on, until the tenth digit is the number of 9s in the number.

SOLUTIONS

TAKE YOUR PICK

C

TEN-DIGIT NUMBER

6210001000

PAINTING A BRIDGE

It would take 4 workers 64 hours to paint a bridge. If another 12 workers help out, how long will it take them all to paint the bridge?

STAMPING

Which stamps, numbered 1, 2, 3, and 4, were used to make pictures A, B, C, and D?

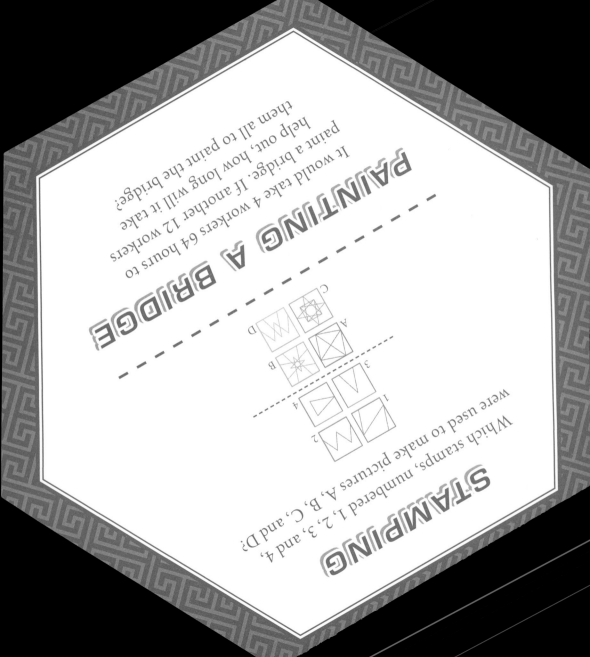

SOLUTIONS

STAMPING

A was printed using stamp 1, B used stamp 3, C used stamp 4, and D used stamps 2 and 3.

PAINTING A BRIDGE

16 hours

Total worker hours needed is 256 (4 x 64).
When split between 16 workers, it will take 16 hours
(256 ÷ 16 = 16).

SIDE VIEW

Which is the correct side view of the blocks:
A, B, or C?

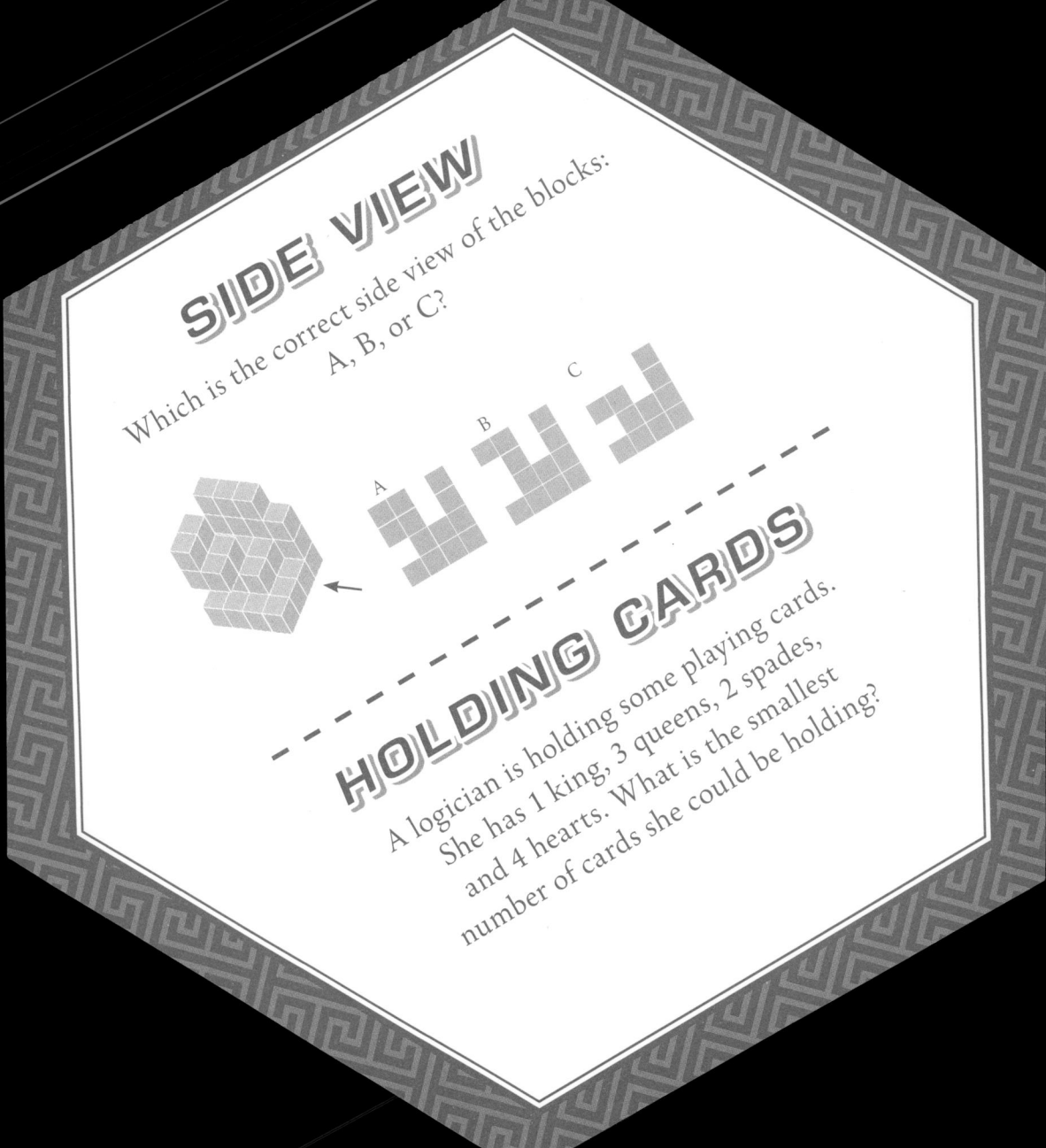

HOLDING CARDS

A logician is holding some playing cards.
She has 1 king, 3 queens, 2 spades,
and 4 hearts. What is the smallest
number of cards she could be holding?

SOLUTIONS

SIDE VIEW

A

HOLDING CARDS

7

There are 4 hearts and 2 spades, making 6 cards. The king could be either of those suits, but since there are 3 queens, there must be a queen from a different suit, making a seventh card.

DOUBLE DIGITS

Find a 2-digit number that is equal
to 9 times the sum of its digits.

NEXT IN LINE

Which shape is next in the sequence: A, B, or C?

A

B

C

?

DOUBLE DIGITS

81

To work this out as an equation,
call the first digit a and the second b:

$$10a + b = 9(a + b)$$
$$10a + b = 9a + 9b$$
$$a = 8b$$

The only 2-digit number whose first
digit is 8 times its second digit is 81.

NEXT IN LINE

A

BAKING MUFFINS

Geraldine has spent the morning baking muffins. She decides to give half of them to her friend George, but only half of that number to her friend Andy. She decides to give a sixth of them to her mother, then keep the last muffin for herself. How many muffins did she bake?

SEE SIDEWAYS

Which is the correct side view of the blocks: A, B, or C?

BAKING MUFFINS

12

George got 6, Andy 3, Mom 2 and Geraldine 1.

SEE SIDEWAYS

B

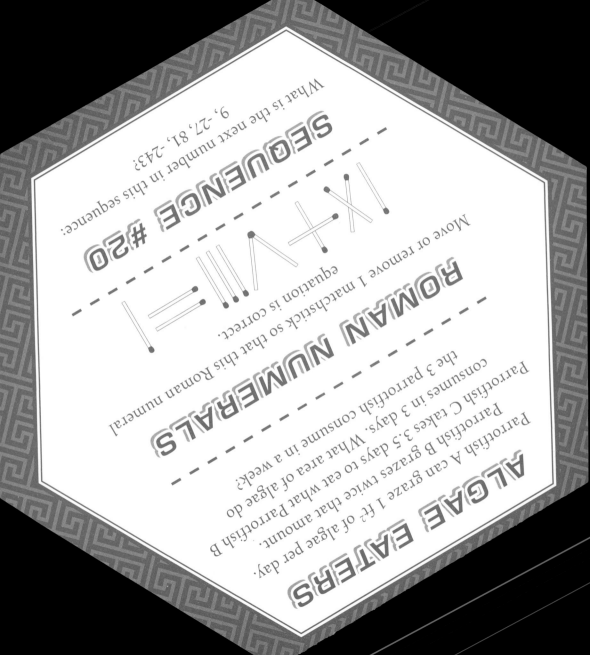

SEQUENCE #20

What is the next number in this sequence:

9, -27, 81, -243?

ROMAN NUMERALS

Move or remove 1 matchstick so that this Roman numeral equation is correct.

IX+VIII=I

ALGAE EATERS

Parrotfish A can graze 1 ft² of algae per day. Parrotfish B grazes twice that amount. Parrotfish C takes 3.5 days to eat what Parrotfish B consumes in 3 days. What area of algae do the 3 parrotfish consume in a week?

SOLUTIONS

ALGAE EATERS

33 ft²

In 7 days, parrotfish A consumes 7 ft² algae, B consumes 14 ft² and parrotfish C consumes 12 ft².

ROMAN NUMERALS

IX−VIII=I

SEQUENCE #20

729

To find the next number, multiply by -3.

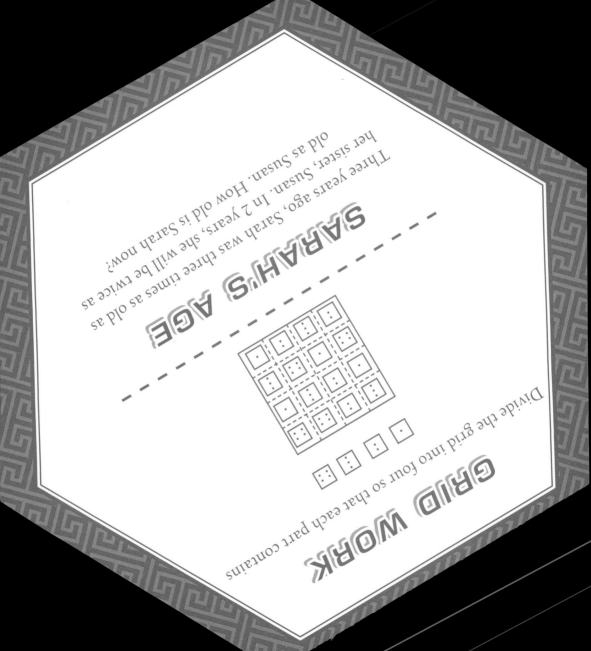

SARAH'S AGE

Three years ago, Sarah was three times as old as her sister, Susan. In 2 years, she will be twice as old as Susan. How old is Sarah now?

GRID WORK

Divide the grid into four so that each part contains

SOLUTIONS

GRID WORK

SARAH'S AGE

18

Three years ago, Sarah was 15 and Susan was 5.
In 2 years, Sarah will be 20 and Susan will be 10.

160

How can four 4s equal 160?

PICK A VIEW

Which is the correct side view of the blocks: A, B, or C?

SOLUTIONS

- - - - - - - - - -

160

$(44 - 4) \times 4 = 160$

- - - - - - - - - - - - - - - - -

PICK A VIEW

A

CAKE BOX

A chocolate cake has been placed in 1 of 4 locked boxes, numbered from left to right. Each box has a key with a different color. Use these clues to discover which box the cake is in and which key will release it:

The black key opens box 3 or 4.

The cake is to the left of the box with a black key.

The orange key opens a box with a black key.

The purple key is to the right of the box with the pink key.

and to the left of the orange key.

The cake is to the right of the black key.

The pink key opens box 1.

SOLUTIONS

- - - - - - - - - -

CAKE BOX

Open box 3 with the purple key to find the cake.

SQUARE SUM

What numbers do these squares and circles represent:

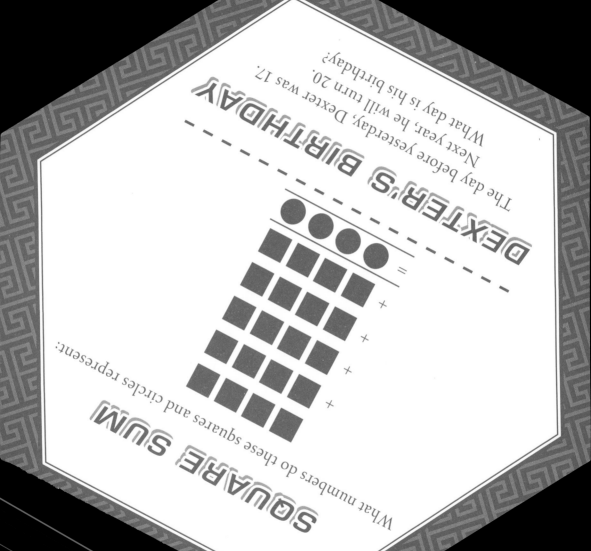

DEXTER'S BIRTHDAY

The day before yesterday, Dexter was 17.
Next year, he will turn 20.
What day is his birthday?

SOLUTIONS

SQUARE SUM

■ = 1 and ● = 5

DEXTER'S BIRTHDAY

December 31

Today, it is January 1 and Dexter is currently 18. He will turn 19 on December 31 this year, and 20 the following year.

SOLVE IT

Correct this equation by moving 1 digit:

104 – 102 = 4

- -

COMPLETE SUIT

How many cards would you need to draw from a
deck of 52 playing cards to be sure of getting
any complete suit?

SOLUTIONS

SOLVE IT

$104 - 10^2 = 4$

COMPLETE SUIT

49

In the worst-case scenario, cards 49, 50, 51 and 52 are the final cards in each of the suits. Since it does not matter which suit you complete, card 49 must complete one of the suits.

MAKE A PATTERN

Which of the patterns A to D cannot be made using stamps 1 to 4?

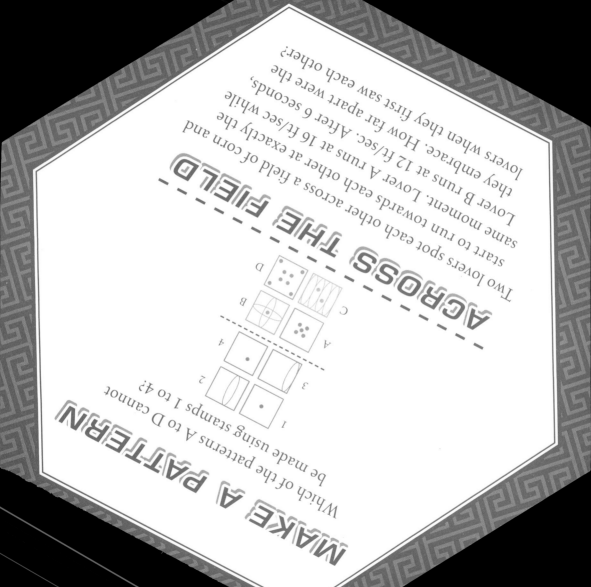

ACROSS THE FIELD

Two lovers spot each other across a field of corn and start to run towards each other at exactly the same moment. Lover A runs at 12 ft/sec while Lover B runs at 16 ft/sec. After 6 seconds, they embrace. How far apart were the lovers when they first saw each other?

SOLUTIONS

MAKE A PATTERN

B and D

ACROSS THE FIELD

168 ft

Lover A covers 96 ft in 6 seconds, while lover B covers 72 ft.

IN THE LIBRARY

There is a dusty row of encyclopedias on a shelf in the library.
If the encyclopedia containing entries J–M is fifth from the left
and fifth from the right, while the encyclopedia containing entries
S–T is seventh from the left, how many encyclopedias are on the shelf?

How can five 7s equal 70?

70

SOLUTIONS

70

$(7 \times 7) + 7 + 7 + 7 = 70$

or

$77 - 7 + 7 - 7 = 70$

IN THE LIBRARY

9

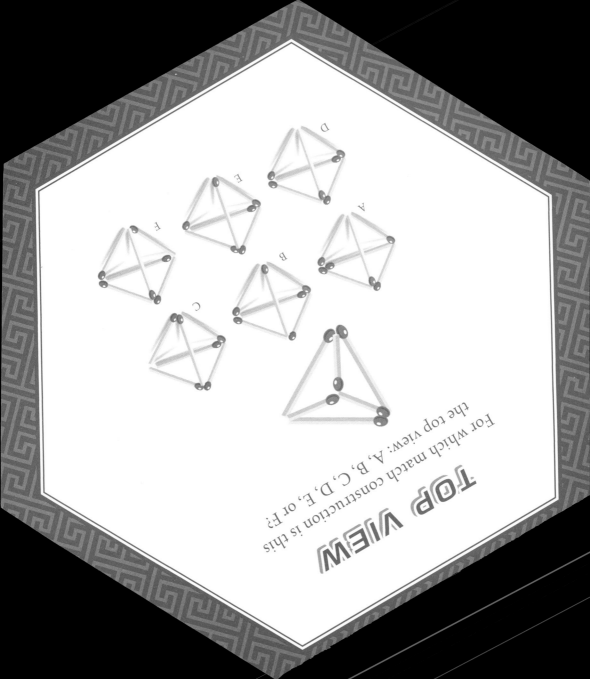

TOP VIEW

For which match construction is this
the top view: A, B, C, D, E, or F?

TOP VIEW

D

T-SHIRT TEST

The geometers Mr. Square, Mr. Circle and Mr. Triangle go out for lunch. Each is wearing a T-shirt with a square, circle, or triangle shape on it. Mr. Square points out that each geometer is wearing a shape that does not match his surname. The geometer wearing the triangle T-shirt laughs, 'Yes, Mr. Square, you are right.' Who is wearing which shape?

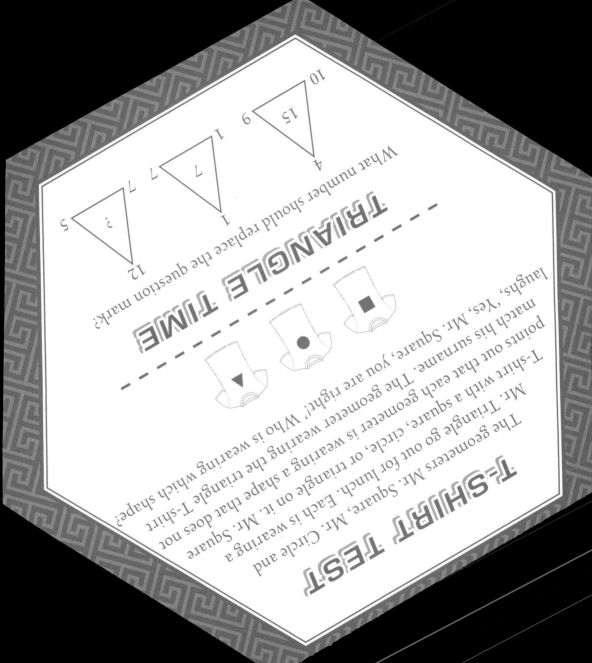

TRIANGLE TIME

What number should replace the question mark?

12 5 ? 7
1 9 7
4 15 10

SOLUTIONS

T-SHIRT TEST

Mr. Square is wearing the circle T-shirt, Mr. Triangle is wearing the square, and Mr. Circle is wearing the triangle.

We know that Mr. Square is not wearing the triangle, so if he is not wearing the square, he must be wearing the circle. The other two geometers must be wearing the remaining shapes that differ from their names.

TRIANGLE TIME

0

The number in the center of each triangle is the sum of the bottom two numbers minus the top number.

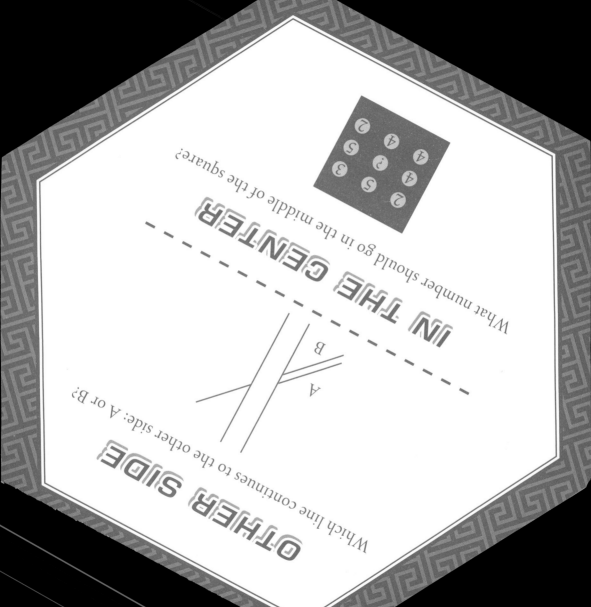

IN THE CENTER

What number should go in the middle of the square?

OTHER SIDE

Which line continues to the other side: A or B?

SOLUTIONS

OTHER SIDE

B

IN THE CENTER

1

Each column and row adds up to 10.